D0042452

The Laws Of
Messiah

From
Love to
Love

Ryuho Okawa

IRH PRESS

Contents

What the Messiah Should Say and Do Now

Showing the Way at the Turning Point of Human History

The Teachings of Messiah

The Battle to Change the Values with Words of God

CHAPTER FOUR

The Heart of the Earth

Shambhala That Promotes Spiritual Awakening of Humanity

CHAPTER FIVE

The Love of Messiah

Love on Earth, the Training Ground for the Souls

Preface

"What is Messiah?" I spoke on this theme before, but here I specifically focused on it. As a matter of fact, this is rather like an interim report, as I am still on my way to my final destination.

At the same time, however, "The Laws of Messiah" is not something that can be taught as one ages closer to death. So, I taught these laws intensively and successively, thinking that I can leave this world at any time.

Here, at 65 years of age, Ryuho Okawa spoke "The Laws of Messiah" (The Laws of Savior).

Ryuho Okawa
Master & CEO of Happy Science Group
November 2021

Now, here, Elohim is thinking about.

Good and Evil Taught by the God of the Earth

1

The Origin of Good and Evil on Earth

This chapter "Now, here, Elohim is thinking about." is based on the 77th lecture I gave in 2021 at Grand Head Temple Shoshinkan as a commemorative talk for Goseitansai (Celebration of Lord El Cantare's Descent). It is a somewhat unusual title and a difficult one.

In the fall of 2021, we released *The Laws of the Universe— The Age of Elohim* [executive producer and original story by Ryuho Okawa] as Part II of the movie series. But Elohim's teachings and thoughts cannot be fully conveyed by imagery alone, so here, I want to organize and share His basic way of thinking. I believe it will serve as a standard for how people today should think in the midst of worry and confusion.

As I wrote in my books, before humankind prospered on Earth, human-type beings lived on Venus when it was not as hot as it is today. Venus is now extremely hot and covered by gas, so it is not habitable by those beings anymore.

Six hundred million years ago, I decided that the next goal would be to establish human civilization on Earth. On Venus, I was called "El Miore," but when coming to Earth, I changed it to "El Cantare."

"El" basically means "God" or "the Light of God." "Cantare" contains the meaning to sing in Latin languages such as Italian and Spanish, but overall, El Cantare means "the Light of the Earth" or "the God of the Earth."

El Cantare began creating human beings on Earth about 600 million years ago, but it was about 330 million years ago when He first put out on earth a physical embodiment of His soul. The name was "Alpha." At Happy Science, I have already taught the Laws of Alpha and described His thoughts and work as the Creator (refer to *The Laws of Alpha*).

The second time El Cantare took on a physical embodiment, His name was "Elohim." "Alpha" and "Elohim" are the names on earth, but the real name is "El Cantare."

He has long guided humankind by the name "Elohim" since appearing on earth about 150 million years ago. So the name Elohim appears in the Old Testament. Some Muslims say that they sometimes say the name Elohim when they pray to Allah. An Uyghur woman who fled to Canada said this too. In an interview she gave when I lectured in Canada, she said, "Instead of saying Allah, we sometimes say Elohim when we pray." So, the name Elohim has been used for quite a long time.

And now, I am once again teaching the Laws for the new era and the foundations for building the next, long history of humankind under the name El Cantare. The teachings are on a vast range of topics, so I do not know how much of them will be passed on to future generations. But some people may want to know various things in detail, so I am giving teachings on a range of topics.

This chapter, "Now, here, Elohim is thinking about." focuses on Elohim, the second incarnation of El Cantare featured in the movie, *The Laws of the Universe—The Age of Elohim*, and the ideas He tried to teach as the basic way of thinking on Earth.

After Elohim's time, various teachings were taught in different countries by those who are called ethnic gods. But the contradictions in these teachings caused wars, discord, inequality, and discrimination. That is why I am here to tell you what the original teachings of the Lord God were.

"The Laws of Alpha" are the Laws of Creator. Alpha taught teachings that were full of hope, such as the purpose for which He gave humans physical bodies to live on earth and what kind of world humans should strive to create. He also taught that to promote evolution, He invited space people from other planets, who could adapt themselves to life on Earth, to live with the Earth-born human race.

The Laws during the age of Alpha, therefore, were about Creation and the co-existence of various life forms from the universe on Earth.

About 180 million years later, in the age of Elohim, the time came when it was necessary to make clear the distinction between good and evil on Earth.

At the time, hell was not a distinct and separate world as it is today. But discord and a sense of who was superior and who was inferior were already growing between people. And after leaving this world, a large number of people wanted to determine their way of life and status in the afterlife based on the values they had while alive on earth.

One of the goals for people on earth was certainly to create wonderful, idealistic societies and make this world a utopia. But this thought of creating ideal societies at times made people forget the original mission they had in the Spirit World. It made many people become attached to their earthly lives, believe that the third dimensional world is the real world, and lose interest in the other world.

Then they started wanting to differentiate themselves in the other world by the differences they had on earth: for example, by whether their position was high or low, whether they were wealthy or not, whether their skin was black, white, or yellow, or whether they were a man or a woman.

Before hell clearly came into existence, in the fourth dimension, people were starting to live separately; some lived in areas that were like higher grounds or hills, whereas others lived in areas that were like the inside of caves or the lower swamplands. Hell gradually began to fully form after this.

You will see this in our movie: about 120 million years ago, Lucifer, the twin brother of Michael, the leader of the Seven Archangels, was born under the name Satan. Lucifer grew jealous of God and was ultimately defeated by his brother, Michael. He said to himself, "Why is it wrong to be jealous of God? What's wrong with me becoming God?" Because he had been enjoying the feeling of being like God on earth, after he died and fell to the underworld, he made himself its overlord. He is the number one devil of hell.

Beneath him, there are many henchmen. What kind of people became devils after death? They were often evil kings or monarchs, religious leaders who led people astray, mistaken philosophers, and people with high status and influence who led many people in the wrong direction. These people are the origins of devils. Under the command of Lucifer, they have been conducting various wrongdoings to expand hell in many countries around the world over a long period of time.

2

The Difficulty of Judging Good and Evil Today When People Have Forgotten God's Laws

When a leader's thinking strays away from God's Will

When you live in this world, it is often hard to know what is good and what is evil.

For example, there are people who are admired for being in a profession that is highly respected in this world, for being from a good family, for being wealthy, or for their good looks. I also understand that there are singers and actors who are greatly admired in today's world. But among the people whom everyone approves of are those who are truly great in the eyes of God and those who are not. Even among the prime ministers of Japan, some return to heaven, whereas others end up in hell.

It is very hard for humanity to tell the difference. This is because people base their judgment not on the Laws of God but on man-made laws or on their own ways of thinking that they developed in this world. These man-made laws or ways of thinking are not always correct.

For the past 200 years, the mass media were expected to play the role of criticizing and, at times, attacking and knocking down bad leaders to prevent evil leaders from emerging. But their work is also a mixture of good and evil, as their judgment is based on the thinking of earthly common sense, knowledge, academic study, and science. So, if such earthly ways of thinking go wrong, the standards of good and evil that are produced by them can also go wrong.

For example, in a certain country, which I won't name, someone considered as the greatest journalist unfortunately fell down to a similar realm in hell as the very opponents he had been criticizing had gone to. So, it is not just angels fighting devils. There are also battles between devils, and this makes it even more difficult these days to tell good apart from evil. In this sense, we are at a very difficult point in time.

It is good that people have faith, pray to God, and think, "What humans create is not always perfect. We may think, 'We should create this kind of political system,' or 'We should create this kind of law,' but we must remember that above the political system and the law exists God or Buddha. Politicians and lawmakers must strive to work on behalf of God and create and enforce systems and laws that reflect God's Will." But this is not how things are today.

Today, democracy, parliamentary systems, political party systems, the rule of law, and other Western ideas of democracy are being accepted as universal values. Nevertheless, some of these values cannot be entirely accepted.

For example, under the rule of law, laws are made by majority vote. The voters are the representatives of the people in this world. So, if the worldly ideas are wrong, or if the majority of people do not pray to God, have wrong thoughts, think only about their interest, or make laws just to their advantage or to maintain their authority, then the laws themselves will have the power to turn this world into hell.

Sadly, neither can electoral democracy be considered a perfect system if the majority of people do not have faith or live in worldly temptations in a way that could make them come under the devil's persuasions.

On the other hand, suppose a single-party dictatorship or autocratic government controls its citizens by forcing on them the idea, "The decisions of the top leader are infallible like God's decisions." Problems can arise if the top leaders' ways of thinking stray away from God's Will. Such leaders can brainwash all their citizens into accepting only one way of thinking, even if the country has hundreds of millions of, or more than a billion, people. They can also grant the citizens freedom except for political matters, and they will not allow the citizens to criticize their leaders.

We see this in China, and we see this in North Korea. In Myanmar too, I think it will soon become impossible to criticize the current military leader. Even in a Buddhist country like Thailand, it is not allowed to criticize the king. This is not just inside the country but outside as well. If you criticize the king abroad, you will be arrested once you go into that country.

When those in power start to preserve themselves by believing that they have the same almighty power as God, then sadly, another hell can form in this world.

The dangers of totalitarianism by the rulers who deny God

I have talked about totalitarianism many times before. One of its characteristics is the tendency to resort to brutal revolution or to rule by violence. Totalitarian regimes take such measures as a matter of course.

They also like to use secret police. They have secret police to control people through different means. Today, these means include wiretapping, tailing, and monitoring with surveillance cameras.

What is more, they have concentration camps. Anyone who is politically inconvenient to them is thrown into a concentration camp, is confined there, and is isolated.

These leaders who deny God will fall to hell and be isolated in Abysmal Hell, where they will not be allowed to communicate with others. They are ideological criminals. If they see others, they will spread their views, so they are left alone in the pitch-black darkness. But in this world, they are the ones who throw their opponents into confinement and lock them up as political criminals in many places. Countries with these characteristics can be considered "totalitarian."

In addition to these, there is another point that should not be forgotten about totalitarian states. Usually, rebellions occur against rulers, but the totalitarian regime always tries to suppress and crush these rebellions. This is their natural reaction. People may imagine that peace will come and stable order will be restored once the rebellions are suppressed and eliminated, but these will never happen. I must make this very clear.

A far more frightening situation will come after the crackdown. It will be worse. Totalitarian states keep creating enemies. They make new enemies one after another. They continue making new enemies and take up a new fight, invade their lands, or destroy them. This is the frightening aspect of them.

Some people may think that revolution is unconditionally good, but I believe the purpose of a revolution should be the establishment of political freedom.

What is political freedom? It is politics that reflects the views of diverse people. It is achieved through discussions between people who are always pursuing "what is right." This is the kind of politics we need.

If more and more countries that have achieved a revolution suppress counter-revolutionary movements and send the protesters to concentration camps or even execute them, then that cannot be called a true revolution; that would instead be "state terrorism."

In particular, when violence becomes blindly permitted, it can lead to ideas such as "The maintenance of the state is the greatest good, and humans should serve the state. Those who defy the state are traitors, so it cannot be helped that they are suppressed." It is easy to arrive at such ideas because this is convenient for those in power. However, it is an extremely dangerous way of thinking.

To make it easier to understand, let me take Hong Kong as an example. Hong Kong is a very small place with only several million residents, but it was the world's third-best financial center. I say it in the past tense because it is now in the past; it "used to be" a financial center.

Economic prosperity cannot be achieved without freedom. When China began making Hong Kong the same as mainland China under the slogan "one country, one system," immediately there arose disorder, repression, and crackdowns on the opposition. This is wrong.

This can only mean that within the leadership in the Beijing government are people who do not understand economic principles. The Chinese Communist Party (CCP) has marked its centenary anniversary and lauds its achievements, but it is still unable to see the mistakes in the communist revolution.

I agree that a society where people are given equality and are freed from a sense of feudal-type hierarchy is a good society. In such a society, all kinds of opportunities and the freedom to succeed are available for all kinds of people. But if one-sided violence and suppression of people's rights and freedom are naturally accepted to achieve equal results for everyone, terrible unhappiness is spreading there.

My point is this: it is impossible to create a utopia by justifying jealousy.

A ruler may be able to make himself look good on the outside, but if he starts to "grind down" every successful person and thinks only about retaining his own power, then people must resist.

In a country, two million people were killed. In this country, intellectuals and those who studied abroad were massacred, and all that was left of them were bones. So, sometimes there are regimes that kill anyone who voices their opinion.

But when something is wrong, you must call it out, even from overseas. If a country dismisses such criticism from abroad as interference in internal affairs and puts their citizens under centralized control and surveillance, then this is an extremely dangerous situation.

3

Japan Must Plan for the Future and Say What Must Be Said

The 20th century was an age of wars and revolutions, but the 21st century could also see a fearful future of a different kind. So, now is the time to organize and correct our ways of thinking.

This is because the times have changed. With the development of computers, various tasks can now be processed very quickly. But if companies only focus on making a profit and think, "We just need to produce things that sell well and bring money," they could be doing wrong on a much larger scale.

For example, in mainland China, there is about one surveillance camera for every two citizens. But the parts used in these surveillance cameras are mostly made in Japan, so they are practically made by Japanese companies. These companies must consider how their products are ultimately used.

Certainly, it was good to have created jobs at factories for the Chinese citizens who had been living in poverty for a long time. It was good that they experienced economic growth.

But recently, the French government imposed sanctions on a Japanese company that makes its products in the Uyghur autonomous region, where people are forced into labor by the Chinese government. The company sells those products for its "low price, low margin, high volume" business. Meanwhile, the Japanese government continues to meander and evade the issue.

It may be difficult to separate politics and economy. But considering Japan's power and its influential voice to speak out on the world stage, it should clearly voice what is right and what is wrong.

It is good that foreign investment comes in and creates new jobs to realize many people's economic prosperity, but it should be done only under the condition that citizens are not subdued under violence, tormented, oppressed, or treated less than human. People must not be treated this way.

In the United States, during Abraham Lincoln's time, the Civil War broke out to protect property rights. In the South, black people were made to do the work of picking cotton and were not treated as human beings.

People in the South saw black people as part of their property that was necessary for developing their cotton plantations, so they fought the war. Abraham Lincoln did not want to have Americans fight each other, but he thought about what justice was and concluded that it was not right to enslave human beings perpetually, so he went to war. Over 610,000 people died in the war, but I think Lincoln is now the most famous god in America.

This shows that at times, you must say what must be said even if you suffer losses. Today, the totalitarianism of the Beijing government has completely repressed Hong Kong. They even froze the assets of a small newspaper company called Apple Daily, preventing it from printing. They did this brazenly while the world was watching, and they claim any criticism against it is interference in internal affairs.

If peace, order, and a safer world are established by making Hong Kong like the other regions under Beijing's rule, then I can understand what they are doing. But judging by the tendencies of totalitarianism, taking control of Hong Kong will make them want to go for Taiwan next. I'm sure it will happen. After that, they will want the Senkaku Islands, Okinawa, the islands and mainland of the Philippines, and Vietnam as well. To achieve that, Beijing already has the military regime in Myanmar under control. They are steadily laying the groundwork.

While knowing this, for example, the Biden administration was formed. They took office because democracy in the United States often sways like a pendulum, but after six months, they realized that they were mistaken and now admit that Mr. Trump was right. They are beginning to change their policies.

They used to dismiss what Mr. Trump said as "conspiracy theories." They accused him of making up the idea that he was conspired against. But now they regret it and are making decisions as the true America would. Even so, the United States did make a mistake and has regressed as a result.

I hope that from now on the United States will function as a healthy nation.

Unfortunately, the Japanese government has a similar problem. I sincerely hope that they stop implementing policies that give them credit only during their terms and adopt a more universal way of thinking, a way of thinking that they believe is right from the perspective of 10 years, 20 years, or even further ahead.

4

Realize the Dangers of Totalitarianism and Fight for Freedom in the 21st Century

Warning 1 During the coronavirus pandemic, Japan's policymakers learned they can restrict people's rights

Sandwiched between the United States and China, Japan is starting to show totalitarian tendencies. In the last one or two years, its policymakers have learned that they can restrict people's rights with just a single word from the top.

They can crush a certain business sector, issue a "stay at home" order, or prohibit people from moving across prefectures. For example, it's a little like martial law, but Tokyo issued a new "state of emergency" the day after I gave this lecture. So, my audience who traveled from Tokyo to Tochigi prefecture could be looked at coldly, as if they were coming to spread germs in Tochigi.

Once a politician gets used to wielding this kind of authority, it's hard for them to stop. It's one form of power. But it bears similarities to how the Beijing government thinks, so we must watch out.

We can accept what should be accepted within reason, but we must resist if this becomes the norm too easily and politicians begin to think they can do anything they want.

When Japan issued the third state of emergency, watching plays was allowed, but going to movie theaters in buildings with floor areas larger than 1,000 square meters (about 10,800 square feet) was not allowed. But when a couple of movie directors made a complaint, which was unusual for the Japanese, the restriction was lifted.

Obedience is one of the virtues of Japanese people, but if you find something is wrong, you must speak up. Don't stay silent and take it. If you think it is wrong, you should speak up and say, "Not a single coronavirus cluster infection occurred in movie theaters, so why should the movie showing be restricted?"

Right now, the government is oversupplying money and granting many subsidies just to get through these times. But if we're not careful, what will come next might be a great recession or a tragedy in certain industries. Even if people can get by for the time being, they might not be able to make it to the end.

But the worst is that humans hate other humans. People are beginning to hate each other. One of the principles of economy is that the economy develops when people buy products or use and receive services. But this principle is being shaken from its very core. It is beginning to seem like it is a good thing for humans to alienate each other and to dislike seeing each other.

At the time, there may be convenient things to make this happen, but there are things that should not be welcomed as convenient.

For example, when I gave this chapter's lecture, it was prohibited to hold an event at a venue with a capacity of more than 10,000 people. So I gave it at Grand Head Temple Shoshinkan and broadcasted it live via satellite. It's good that people can watch my lecture via satellite transmission, but if this situation continues, the government can possibly prevent particular groups from gathering. We need to be aware of this danger.

Warning 2 The rise of AI totalitarianism and surveillance capitalism

• The monitoring with cameras and drones conducted in China

Another change we are seeing since we entered the 21st century is the rise of what is called artificial intelligence (AI) totalitarianism. Not enough understanding and judgment have been made on this topic.

AI is processing massive amounts of data to make decisions for us. I said that in China, there is one surveillance camera for every two citizens. They also have drones in the air.

If, for example, someone is not wearing a mask, the drone can identify their face. The drone takes a photo of them, and then the arrest comes. And if they are taken away to a concentration camp somewhere, even their family members won't have any idea what happened to them. This is what can happen. This is a level at which the government has most probably crossed the line. It is highly likely that this counts as a human rights violation.

In terms of AI totalitarianism, I hesitate to say this because people working at AI-related companies are probably making profits, but we should not just be happy with this technology. It must not go so far as to violate human rights. We must know this.

• The power of mega-corporations to silence even the president of the United States

This is a similar term, but some people say that the age of "surveillance capitalism" has begun.

This is not just about China. This can be seen in the United States, it is seen in Japan, it exists in China, and it is happening elsewhere. It is done by mega-corporations such as GAFA—Google, Apple, Facebook (Meta), Amazon.

These giant companies that command information across the world have huge convenience in an age like today, so they are profiting tremendously. Some areas have increased their tax revenues thanks to them. Companies such as GAFA can centrally control all their customers' information via electronic data, which is called "surveillance capitalism," and their appearance means that a new power has arisen.

The world is yet to make a judgment on this point from a larger perspective.

In a particular example, in the last U.S. presidential election, and even now, a certain company chose not to air the comments of the incumbent president or the former president. This means that the company has gained power similar to the legislative branch of the government.

To speak more clearly, when Mr. Trump was the sitting president, his Twitter account was suspended. He moved to Florida after his term in office, but Facebook (social media) decided to suspend his account for two years, basically until the end of the midterm election. This benefits a certain political party but not the others.

How this decision was made is not clear. Was it decided by the top executive after a company-wide consensus through discussions? Or was it decided by a mere chief-level staff member who was in charge? It is not clear who has the authority.

• My firsthand experience seeing free speech suppressed in Hong Kong

Some people say that China started to oppress Hong Kong just recently, but that's not true.

I have spoken about this before. I went to Hong Kong in 2011 and gave a lecture ("The Fact and The Truth") during a typhoon. The night before the lecture, I arrived at my hotel and saw the Happy Science animation movie, *The Laws of Eternity* [executive producer, Ryuho Okawa, 2006], aired on TV. This airing was perhaps arranged by our Hong Kong branch. While I was watching it, the moment it came to the scene of the Spirit World and its explanation, the screen suddenly blacked out. It didn't show anything after that.

That was in 2011, even before Xi Jinping took full power. The TV blacked out when the scene of the Spirit World came on. It was already happening in Hong Kong three years before the Umbrella Revolution. This is a characteristic of a totalitarian country, so we must be well aware of this.

I believe it's important to loathe and strongly reject a nation that controls information and does not allow its citizens to speak up unless they are loyal to the government.

Founding freedom and creating a society where people can make the right choice between good and evil

Why is the foundation of freedom essential? Freedom can give birth to evil, but utilizing freedom allows everyone to know what is good and bad and make the right choice—this is important.

Take clothes, for example. New styles are always coming out, but it is up to the people to try on different pieces and choose what looks good on them. Good products will sell more, whereas bad products will disappear. The same is true with comics; good ones will spread, whereas some bad ones should be weeded out.

Humans have been given the freedom to decide it through competition in a free market. So, we must leave enough room for that.

Back in 1991, Happy Science got a little offended and protested in what we call "The Friday War." Happy Science religion had only just gained its legal status at the time, but a Japanese weekly magazine *Friday* used their power of publishing and reporting to severely and one-sidedly attack us out of their misunderstanding.

As I think about it now, I can say that there are sometimes truths in what gets reported in the weekly magazines or sports papers that are not generally highly regarded. For example, sports and evening papers run stories about UFO sightings, alien encounters, or people seeing ghosts, but major national newspapers hardly ever report such stories. Major national TV networks also rarely feature them. They report negative news and avoid anything that has to do with spiritual matters or extraterrestrial beings.

Is this right or wrong? I would say that it is not necessarily right.

In the United States, the Department of Defense issued a report on the 144 sightings of UFOs. It said one of them was a balloon, but the other 143 were still unclear. It said they could be unknown weapons from other countries but did not rule out the possibility of space people. It's a difficult matter to dig into.

The Japanese government is still empty-headed, avoiding weighing in, and it only echoes the news; but we at Happy Science have been disclosing this type of information.

Existing authorities and institutions are unable to shed light on this unknown matter, and they tend to hide the truth. So, there are times when we must be resolute and fight.

5

Savior's Work Is Heavy in an Age of Eight Billion People

Humankind should have faith and listen to God's voice

People around the world have different ways of thinking depending on their religion or their legal system, so it is very hard to bring these different ways of thinking together. But it has been a part of Earth's history to accept this diversity to some extent, so I would like to continue doing so. I just want you to tell people around the world that the value judgment I am teaching should be the foundation of how to think.

I have been giving many important messages, but unfortunately, they are still not reaching enough people. I truly wish to somehow tell the Truth to many people.

I have already pointed out that many mistakes are being made by communist one-party dictatorships and autocracies, but Western-style democracy is beginning to show many dangerous traits, too. Moreover, in more and more countries, power is being seized through military coup d'états.

In places where violence is dominant, can people's voices triumph over guns? There is the saying, "The pen is mightier than the sword," but in reality, a sword is stronger than a pen and a gun is stronger than a sword. So, the future will be very harsh if you accept the ideas, "It's OK to use weapons and kill however many people if it is for the sake of a revolution" and "Control information, and it will be as if nothing happened."

In democratic societies, too, some places are becoming totalitarian; people are homogenizing their views on human rights issues and climate change issues. Here, too, I intend to say what must be said if I sense any danger.

Yes, there are differences between men and women. If people become too liberal regarding this issue, this world can turn into a difficult place to live in.

When El Cantare created human beings, He separated them into men and women. This is the policy on Earth. Some people are changing their views because people's sexes can now be artificially altered using biological or medical technology, but we also need to consider if it's the right choice from their soul's perspective.

Of course, human rights are important, but if people become too liberal, they too can fall into the hands of devils.

So, please have faith first.

Listen to God's words.

Please do not disregard the wisdom that humanity has accumulated over a long period of time.

Science and material prosperity can be accepted based on these, but this world is not the final home for human beings.

It is just a training ground for the soul.

Please remember this, and seek the wisdom to choose what is right from the diversity of values. It is also our work to preserve this Earth so that we can continue to use it for a long time as a training ground to refine such wisdom.

My work as Savior to correct humanity's mistaken ways of thinking

I know that the truth about the afterlife is not yet widely known, but I want the Happy Science teachings to reach every corner of the Earth. It is taking a while to do so, but we already have members in over 160 countries.

Our power will not be enough if it is only from Japan.

If a seed is planted in your country, please make it sprout and bloom there.

Spread it to tens of thousands, to hundreds of thousands, to millions of people, and help them grow.

There are things we cannot do as we wish. In India, for example, we have a lot of members, but it is very hard to build a center or facility that can connect everyone there. Transferring money from Japan, for example, is sometimes difficult. Each country has its own conditions.

So, I ask the people around the world to make the effort to do what they can to spread the teachings.

And in light of the information Happy Science puts out, if you find something wrong in the current politics and economy or in the work done by the mass media, make a change by voicing your opinion.

If you think something is wrong, say that it is wrong.

As for Japan, the prime minister has been hoping that the vaccines would solve everything and the Olympics would be a great success, but things are not going as he wishes. The struggle will continue.

But we must overcome these tough times. I will keep on fighting based on the principle of protecting the people with faith.

All of you, now, here, please listen.
Don't be defeated by coronavirus-related issues.
These come from materialism,
So, now we must have a strong mind.
Please spread this message.

Now, the world population is almost eight billion people.
If more than half of them, the majority,
Have wrong thoughts,
Or, in other words,
If they are trying to create a world without faith,
This will invite a repercussion.
So, before it happens,

I truly want to change humanity's way of thinking.
I believe this is the work of the Savior.

My work this time is heavy.
The world is large with so many countries.
Also, at a time like this when a virus is widespread,
We cannot travel freely.
But even so, come what may,
Our teachings must prevail through it and spread.
I believe so.
Please build up your life and work
With faith as your main pillar.
And spread to as many people as possible
The right way of living as human beings.

CHAPTER
TWO

What the Messiah Should Say and Do Now

Showing the Way
at the Turning Point of Human History

1

Looking Back on the 20th Century, the Age When the Modern Messiah Was Born

This chapter will be as difficult as Chapter One, "Now, here, Elohim is thinking about." It's called "What the Messiah Should Say and Do Now." Coming from me, this chapter is very hard to talk about. Frankly, I should talk about the future in the way the Book of Revelations does, but as I am now living, working, and still active, I cannot simply speak in the way of the Revelations and give prophecies matter-of-factly.

One way to put it is if the people in the year 1900 were asked the question, "What will the 20th century be like?" I don't think many people would be able to give an accurate prediction.

How many people were able to foresee World War I and World War II, the Russian Revolution and communist revolutions, the formation and the collapse of the Soviet Union, and Germany's defeat in World War I and their remilitarization 20 years later that led to the start of World War II? I also don't think anyone expected that the United Nations, formed by the nations that won World War II, would split into two factions, as it has now, and fail to function.

I heard there was a prophecy that the Soviet Union would come to an end in 76 years. But the situation today is that the Chinese Communist Party has celebrated its 100th anniversary since its founding and is planning to make more leaps. At the same time, different views about totalitarianism are emerging. For example, I read in today's newspaper that a new Russian law will be enacted to forbid Stalin's Soviet government from being compared with the Nazi Germany fascism. This is because they are essentially enemies, as Germany would not have been defeated if the Soviet Union had not joined the war. Due to this new law, freedom of speech and academic freedom will be restricted.

We are now entering a time of difficulty. There will also be times when each country may insist on their legitimacy and deny or look down on views that oppose theirs.

We just took a look from the year 1900. What if we now look back from the year 2000? What kind of era was the 20th century when we look at it from the year 2000? If we could redo it, what should we have done, where, and how? Finding the answers to "What could we have done differently?" is extremely difficult.

For example, at the time of World War I, fighter planes were propeller planes with two fixed wings or biplanes. At first, no one had thought of using them as a weapon. When a pilot crossed paths with an enemy in the air, they waved at each other in greeting. This was World War I.

But by World War II, bombers and fighter planes were in use. Combat planes battled each other and against aircraft carriers, battleships, destroyers, and submarines. Many new things started happening, and in just 20 years, the concept of war changed.

Aside from World Wars I and II and revolutions, another perspective to consider when looking back to the 20th century from the year 2000 is the invention of and attack via atomic bombs on Hiroshima and Nagasaki. This incident is one of the events that should be recorded in the history of the current civilization that spans from the past 2,000 and a few hundred years up to about 3,000 years.

This was when humankind saw what happens when a nuclear weapon is used for the first time in real life. It showed that the attackers can destroy an entire city and either kill or wound most of its population without having to stain their hands with blood—all in just a blink of an eye. No one can imagine the amount of guilt the pilot who pushed the button and dropped the bomb felt. He probably felt some guilt, but he must also have been decorated by his country for his action. So, it may have been hard to know if his actions were good or evil until he died.

Another incident similar to this is the air raids, like the one on Tokyo, in which as many as 100,000 people died in a single night when their homes were firebombed. People jumped into the Kanda River to escape the blaze or were burned to death.

Anyone who had watched this whole scene for a while would recognize that it was the Hell of Agonizing Cries.

After Hiroshima and Nagasaki, no one has been able to use atomic bombs. For example, in the Cuban Missile Crisis of 1962, when President Kennedy learned that the Soviet Union would deliver nuclear missiles to Cuba by sea, the young president ordered a naval quarantine, surrounded Cuba with U.S. naval ships, and said that he would not hesitate to go to war if the line was crossed. The crisis continued until the eleventh hour.

Someone studying in America at the time said, "It felt as if a nuclear war between the United States and the Soviet Union could happen at any moment. It was terrifying." But the horrors of Hiroshima and Nagasaki were still fresh in the minds of the world leaders then. So, they turned the Soviet ships around, and the nuclear missile sites were taken down. What could have been a full-scale war between the United States and the Soviet Union was averted at the last moment.

I believe this was a kind of "challenge." If Kennedy had been weak-minded, the nuclear missiles would have reached Cuba and the bases would have been built. If Cuba had launched nuclear missiles on several cities in America, I don't think America would have been able to prevent all missiles from hitting them.

A similar situation is happening today too. If South Korea or Japan is targeted by North Korea's nuclear missile, they probably wouldn't be able to shoot it down completely. The same is true if China launched one.

This shows that when a tragedy occurs, humankind will remember it for a while, but after a while, the memory of it can fade away.

2

History of Intrusion
by the Strong Countries and
How Messiahs Acted at the Time

Historical examples of how the weak lost in battle

Today's struggle is also said to be between democracy and autocratic-despotism. In ancient times, when Greece and Persia were at war, Persia had an enormous autocratic government and many armies. Greece lost in battle after battle, to the point that most of Greece was burned down by Persian forces. They had to flee on boats, so there was a time when Greece was said to exist only on boats floating in the Mediterranean.

The tables turned after a naval battle, but until then, they lost every battle on land. Even mighty Sparta, a part of Greece, was completely defeated in battle. As depicted in the movie *300*, it was an insane battle of 300 men against 200,000 or 300,000 Persian soldiers. Those 300 men may be heroes, as they fought in a land battle that they had no chance of winning from the beginning.

What this means is that even Greece, with Athens and Sparta, did not stand a chance on land against a war of aggression commanded by a dictator of a huge autocratic nation. However, the tides turned in the battle on the Mediterranean because Persia was not strong at sea.

On another occasion, at around 4 B.C.—according to current religious historians—Jesus Christ was born and tried to save the world. But after three years of missionary work that he started at the age of 30, he was captured by the Jews, was accused of "pretending to be God and spreading a false religion," was perhaps treated just like other criminals, and was put to death on the cross.

But by around 70 A.D., the Jewish kingdom also perished. Massacred at the siege of Masada, the kingdom was lost, and its people scattered all over the world. For 1,900 years, they lived as diaspora, dispersed people, sustaining themselves by working in finance, business, and trade with just their faith in the Old Testament.

Then, in 1948, Israel became a nation again for the first time in 1,900 years. It was built on the corner of Palestine out of guilt for the genocide, mass murder, of six million Jews in Poland by the Nazis during the war, with backing from mainly England, France, and the United States.

While this was a salvation to the people who had fled from country to country with no land to call home, it also produced the possibility of new conflicts. The country was built by forcing a partition on a land that Arabs, or Palestinians, were already living on. This means that the past owners' rights to the land were taken away, so they would of course want to try and get the land back somehow.

On the other hand, what Israel learned from experiencing the genocide by Hitler was that no matter how developed your culture is, if you don't have a military, you can perish.

Only a fraction of the Jews who fled Germany to France survived. Some survived by being taken in by churches. But the majority of the survivors were the ones who fled to England and then to the United States when the war situation of England worsened. These people then helped the postwar United States significantly prosper. In that way, the Jews proved that they are very capable, but they also showed that you can perish even if you excel as a people.

Israel vs. Islamic countries, a battle between a nation that defends itself with nuclear arms and nations that oppose it

When Israel was founded in 1948, political theorist Hannah Arendt realized that this could lead to trouble. She was able to tell that this would start another war. She herself was a German-born Jew who escaped to the United States through France, but she foresaw that the creation of a new country will start a war. As predicted, the Middle East War occurred and went on until the Fourth Arab-Israeli War. I remember her saying she was relieved that Israel won. She probably thought Israel's defeat was unavoidable. This is because it is very difficult to establish a country where it didn't exist before and to fight the nations that are already there.

That is why Israel is militarily a very powerful nation. They are said to be the fourth most powerful in the world—sometimes even second. They don't disclose their nuclear capabilities, so we don't know clearly, but they are thought to be that powerful.

Why did Israel become so powerful? When Iran was experiencing a wave of Islamic fundamentalism after toppling the monarchy in a counter-revolution, their rallying call was "Wipe Israel off the face of the Earth." The idea was that "Peace will never come unless Israel is annihilated."

But, unfortunately, the official Islamic states are not always in agreement with one another; nor do they always get along. They are divided into two big factions, the Sunni and Shiah, and many smaller factions that are associated with guerilla organizations, so they are struggling to be unified.

Developed countries fear that if Iran possesses nuclear weapons and becomes a major power, it may lead other Islamic nations under the banner of destroying Israel. So they are intervening the best they can and making the six-nation agreement.

During President Trump's term, the United States sided with Israel and claimed that the Golan Heights belonged to Israel. And to flatter Trump, the Israeli prime minister said to him, "Let's call this area Trump Heights." There was such an interaction going on.

Now, a new administration is in power and things are in flux. The future is unclear.

The leading country among the Islamic nations until a short while ago was Iraq. But after it was defeated by the United States in the Iraq War, Iran has been aiming to fill the seat. The possession of nuclear weapons may help them, but the other Islamic nations are watching attentively and trying to prevent it from happening.

From their point of view, "It is we who are the indigenous people. It is unfair that Israel, which was artificially created later, is armed with nuclear weapons. They can destroy us, but we can't destroy them. This should not be allowed, both in terms of defense and also by the population size."

Israel's population is not even 10 million. Even if you include the Jews living abroad, the population would still be no more than 15 or 20 million, which is less than Taiwan's population. I can imagine that the Islamic nations find it difficult to accept that such a country is in control of the life and death of their country.

Prophets that appeared in the tragic history of Jewish people, who were at the mercy of stronger countries

• Moses

Now, if we take a look from the perspective of the Israeli people, they have suffered a number of tragedies throughout their history.

You will find that the Old Testament, which precedes the teachings of Jesus in the New Testament, is about how Israel established their race and protected their people, how God is protecting them because they are God's chosen people, and how prophets were sent to Israel one after another.

Even a country like this has experienced many tragedies. I understand if you have forgotten your world history classes, but Israel was first founded around the time Jews became slaves of Egypt. It is said that they were enslaved and were made to build pyramids for hundreds of years.

Moses, who was of Jewish descent, was placed in a basket and sent down a river, as he was destined to be killed; he was coincidently picked up by a princess in the royal court who had no children of her own and was raised as an Egyptian.

When he was around 20 years old, he learned that he was a Jew, the same people who were being treated as slaves and killed as they performed the treacherous work of building the pyramids. Then, eventually, he realized his mission and led the Exodus.

The official statement is that 600,000 adult males completed the Exodus. In addition, women, children, and animals accompanied them to escape; so if you look at it numerically, it is estimated that there were about two million people in total.

The story from here is very mythical, so I cannot state it clearly, but although Egypt just watched and allowed this group of two million people to escape on foot or by drawing their donkeys in the beginning, they later changed their minds. The Egyptians chased after them, and that is when, it is said, "The Red Sea split into two to allow the group to cross." And when Moses and his people made it across the sea, it closed in, drowning the army of the pharaoh or the Egyptian king.

This story has been considerably modified by the later people, so it's questionable whether everything worked out as well as they say it did. In addition, as the modern Red Sea is so deep, there are assumptions that maybe the story was influenced by various other stories because it is hard to believe the waters parted.

Further north of the sea is a shallower lake. There are times when you can see the bottom. Some scholars say,

"When the strong east wind blows, you can sometimes see the bottom, so maybe that's what they are talking about. Maybe it's not the Red Sea but a sea of reeds." My view is closer to that, but there are all kinds of embellishments to the beginning story of any ethnic group's history, so I believe it is not right to say this or that about it.

Even though Moses and his group experienced such a great happening by the power of God's miracle, they wandered the desert for decades in search of the "land flowing with milk and honey," the paradise or Utopia that God had promised them.

As they continued wandering across the desert, occasionally they would find an oasis and take temporary shelter there. And when they finally arrived in the land promised to them by God, a different group of people was already living there.

As you can see, what we are experiencing right now has already happened during the Exodus, more than 3,000 years ago. The land that God had promised them was already inhabited by other people and this led to war.

Moses was not able to reach it because he died before he could, so Joshua led the people in. But in the end, a war happened, and their nation ended up being built by plundering the land.

• Jeremiah

Thus, when you read the Old Testament, all you see is a history of wars between countries. War after war is repeated. That is why, in Jewish history, "the Messiah" is known to be the one who appears in order to save the kingdom from destruction.

The one who protects the people and preserves the kingdom is called the Messiah. However, at times, it was not possible to protect everyone, such as when the Babylonian captivity occurred.

After all, the civilization in the Tigris-Euphrates basin was the more ancient and stronger one. Just as the Jews were enslaved by the Egyptians, they once again became captives, this time in Babylon, were taken to the capital of Iraq, and were made slaves there. Israel effectively became a colony.

It was prophet Jeremiah who warned them time after time that there would be an attack from the north. It is pretty much the same story as that of Nichiren[1], who later in Japan during the Kamakura period warned about the Mongolian invasion but was persecuted and almost put to death by the Shogunate government; in the end, he was exiled to Sado Island. Likewise, Jeremiah's warnings also went unheard. The invading army came, and the Jews were held in the Babylonian captivity.

Jeremiah was captured and lowered into a well by a rope. The bottom of the well was filled with mud. I think there was water too, but he was sunk into the mud all tied up in rope and was left to hang there. It was very much like torture. This was what he had to go through.

What did he gain out of it? Enemies besieged the city, so his prophecy did come true. But in the end, he was just released and was able to live. That was all. He could not save his country. His prophecy of doom was accurate, but it did not save his people.

What they should have done was listen to God's words, respond to Jeremiah's call, and bolster its defense to prevent the invasion. But already 2,600 years ago, people did not believe in the words of God that Jeremiah was relaying.

• Jesus

Jesus Christ was born 500 or 600 years later, around the beginning of the first century. What Jesus did was also the same.

A verse in the prophecy of the First Isaiah in the Old Testament states, "The Messiah will appear and save Israel," though it is not clear about when it would happen.

The Bible states, "The Messiah will come into Jerusalem riding on a donkey, greeted by shouts of 'Hosanna, hosanna!'" "And the Son of Man will be crucified."

In terms of the series of Jesus Christ's last actions, people say that he acted according to the words of the Old Testament in order to fulfill them.

But it is also a fact that many of his disciples were opposed to him entering Jerusalem only to be put on the cross. Such is reality.

As for how the Jews view Jesus, they have come to recognize him as one of the prophets but not as the Savior.

Even before Jesus' time, Rome was a massive nation, and Israel was but a small colony, so it stood no chance of winning against Rome. Its government was a puppet government under Rome, and only the people who followed traditional Judaism that got along with the Roman government were protected by Rome for keeping a look out for any groups from emerging as a new rebel using the power of religion. This was the situation at the time. Knowing this will allow you to understand the general storyline of the New Testament.

China's threat that can be seen in their suppression of freedom of religion and freedom of speech

The same thing is happening in China.

There are many Christians in China. Official numbers put them at 100 million. If you include underground believers, it is said that they number as many as 200 million.

The Beijing government and the Vatican are in conflict over who has the right to appoint the Catholic bishops, but the Vatican, which does not possess military powers, is relenting and allowing the appointment of those approved by the Chinese government.

China's constitution promises freedom of religious belief and freedom of speech, but in reality, these rights are not protected. This is because they believe, "If you are not a patriot, then you are not a citizen."

A similar kind of thinking existed in Japan at the time of World War II. The term was "Hikokumin," and it meant that "anyone who opposes the war is a betrayer. They are not citizens of this country."

When people are framed to think that you must be a patriot and love your country, it would be a matter of course that freedom of speech, freedom of the press, and freedom of religion are suppressed and cracked down on.

The Vatican is one of the few nations that recognize Taiwan as a sovereign state. So, China may be making the Vatican suffer to put pressure on Taiwan.

In this way, similar situations have arisen many times throughout history.

3

The Impact Atomic Bombings Have Had on Humankind

Looking back at World War II from the year 2000 and pondering the "Ifs" of history

If we were to redo our history from the year 2000, there would be several things we shouldn't have done if we had known that China would become massively powerful as it has now. Many mistakes were made by postwar historians, journalists, and politicians.

What would we see if we looked at it from the United States' perspective, who now sees China as a potential adversary?

During the war, before Japan's Kamikaze units, the United States' Doolittle raiders flew with only enough fuel to fly one way, dropped their bombs over Tokyo, Nagoya, Osaka, Kobe, and other Japanese cities, and then belly-landed in China. It was a tactic that took the Japanese military by surprise. It is said that most of them belly-landed in China because they were out of fuel.

To them, these were heroic acts. They were also heroic acts for the United States as a country because they helped China. However, several decades later, China is becoming the United States' greatest threat. Considering this, it must now be difficult for them to evaluate the acts.

With regard to dropping atomic bombs on Japan, the explanation that has long been given is that it was necessary to end the war early. There are also theories that if the war had continued, the Soviets might have advanced south and seized Hokkaido and the Tohoku area of northern Japan. These are all "ifs" of history, so it's hard to say.

Talked into by Churchill, the Soviet Union defeated Germany at a tremendous cost—they lost 20 million lives. So, as "souvenirs" to make up for their loss, many states were turned into pro-Soviet communist satellites. But from Japan, all they got were four islands, what Japan terms the Northern Territories. For this reason, Russia is averse to letting go of these "rewards of the war." Negotiations on this are still in a deadlock today.

This often happens. In history, an event that was once celebrated can become the opposite. The victor can trigger the next misfortune, and the defeated can become more aggressive and fight back more ferociously.

Furthermore, the atomic bombings of Hiroshima and Nagasaki had the effect of foreshadowing a change in how wars would be fought around the world. The Soviet Union led the arms race with their hydrogen bomb test. Then the United States followed, and now all five permanent member countries of the U.N. Security Council have hydrogen bombs. North Korea is not a member, but they claim that they have both atomic and hydrogen bombs, demonstrating that once a country has one, attacking them becomes difficult.

In light of such historical uncertainties, what if we looked back on the 21st century from the standpoint of the year 2100? What will happen, and can it be changed? I would like to talk about this perspective in this chapter as well.

The aftereffects of atomic bomb
1) Intervention from outer space that started in earnest

The atomic bombings of Hiroshima and Nagasaki changed warfare. But there were two more impacts.

One impact was that intervention from outer space started in earnest as a result of the use of atomic bombs.

It's the so-called Roswell Incident that took place in the United States in 1947. It is said that a flying saucer crash-landed in New Mexico, and its spaceship and extraterrestrial occupants—some dead, but some still alive—were recovered. This has been kept secret for a very long time.

After that, the number of UFO sightings shot up. The United States has the highest number but many sightings are happening in developed countries and other places. Many UFOs were seen in Mexico and South America as well. In the case of Japan, the number of reports had been very small, but sightings have significantly increased during recent years.

One showed up in China and forced an airport to cease operations for an hour. An object that clearly appeared to be a UFO came and lit up the airport with bright light. Flights were grounded and the airport was closed off. Russia also has many reports of such sightings.

Not all nations of the world have disclosed the information they have, but many countries are having doubts about whether these are really from outer space or are secret military weapons of other countries.

Even the Nazis were developing UFOs in Hitler's last days—there is actual film footage of the experiments. Recordings show that they got as far as developing an object that floats up as it rotates.

This has led to legends such as, "Hitler never died. He got on a UFO or a submarine and escaped to Antarctica where he now lives somewhere underground." But it is a fact that the Nazis were studying UFOs.

It is also a fact that both Germany and Japan were trying to develop atomic bombs during the war. If there had been a time lag of one or two years, Germany or Japan could have been the ones who used the weapons instead.

Therefore, it can be said that it was time for a new chapter in human history.

Then around the time the Roswell Incident took place—which was two years after the atomic bombings in 1945—space beings made their appearance through the incident. It happened because the number of space beings observing Earth from outer space had increased since the bombings. Also, because the number of fighter planes and commercial airplanes in the air has increased, people are more likely to spot space beings. It has become easier to capture sightings on video or in photographs with the proliferation of cameras. People's interest in outer space is growing.

A recent U.S. report revealed that there have been 144 cases of unidentified flying objects sightings in recent years. One of them was a balloon, but the others remain unexplained. They could be weapons from other countries for spying or attacking, but it can't be ruled out that they belong to aliens. The report ends inconclusively, for now.

But I am sure that behind closed doors, each country is investigating space beings and their involvement from outer space. In some cases, any country that manages to harness for military purposes the technology that allows space beings to travel light-years from far-flung distances has far more advantages. In a way, this would be able to turn the tables completely for any countries in inferior positions.

Japan has been very behind when it comes to information about the universe, so Happy Science has been revealing a lot in the past 10 years. I believe that is also what the space beings want.

Particularly, in 2010, I gave a daytime lecture at Yokohama Arena on "The Opening of the Space Age," and in the last five minutes, I said something like, "The Space Age is about to begin and you will witness many things" (in the El Cantare Celebration lecture "Becoming a World Religion: A Paradigm Shift for Earth People" given on December 4, 2010. See *Secrets of the Everlasting Truths*). After the lecture, when the thousands of people who heard my talk in Yokohama went outside, they saw a UFO fleet of more than 100 spaceships in the air.

This was daytime, not nighttime, so it's clear that they were not stars. It's also clear that they were not U.S. military or Japan Self-Defense Forces aircraft. There were thousands of witnesses. I remember that as I was leaving the Yokohama Arena in a car, many members walking along the road were

The UFO fleet that appeared in the sky above Yokohama Arena, where Ryuho Okawa gave the lecture, "Becoming a World Religion: A Paradigm Shift for Earth People" on December 4, 2010. Thousands of people witnessed the fleet at the same time.

Secrets of the Everlasting Truths (Tokyo: IRH Press, 2012)

looking up and pointing at the sky. There were over 100 spaceships in the so-called UFO fleet. I believe this was the earnest bell ring that signaled the beginning.

Why UFO sightings are on the rise in Japan

The fact that a large fleet of UFOs appeared after I talked about the universe must mean that the lectures I give are reaching the people of the universe. The space beings in the UFOs monitored the lecture I gave in Japanese and could be translating it into their language, or they could understand it telepathically. I'm sure there are different ways.

But at the very least it is certain that they caught the message I was sending out, and when the members came outside after the lecture, they confidently showed themselves in the sky. They boldly appeared in broad daylight on a Saturday midafternoon despite the risk of the SDF and U.S. military bases being nearby—but not for long, of course. I think they flew away in about 10 minutes.

They have the technology to show up and not show up on the radar, so there is nothing the U.S. air force and SDF can do even if they scramble.

Even when flying through the Earth's atmosphere, the normal cruising speed of these UFOs is Mach 2 or 3. They can also rapidly accelerate to Mach 8 or 10. Mach is the speed of sound, so anything faster than the speed of sound is Mach. Ordinary airplanes fly at speeds of several hundred kilometers per hour. Once the speed transcends the "Mach barrier," flying will physically be very tough for human beings on Earth.

Right now, an airplane takes about 13 hours to travel the distance between Japan and the United States. But if the power of a UFO is added, it would take less than 10 minutes to travel halfway around the globe.

Three footage of UFOs, released by the Pentagon under orders of the U.S. president, show them floating in the air, completely unaffected by the 60-meter per second (134 mph) wind. These images are causing a lot of fear because if this is the work of human beings, then a mighty new technology has been created.

These are the speeds at which these spaceships move. If they move at Mach 8 or 10, no missile could hit them. Most missiles cannot reach Mach 2 or 3.

So, to a UFO moving at this speed, even the speed of a launched ICBM (intercontinental ballistic missile) would seem very slow. An ICBM fired at a country on the other side of the world would take about an hour to reach its target. But with UFO technology, it would be possible to shoot it down.

If North Korea or China does fire a missile at Japan, or at a U.S. military base in Japan, it would only take less than 10 minutes for the missile to hit its target. And to counter it, Japan says that the missiles can be promptly detected by their various reconnaissance vessels and be intercepted with PAC-3s; however, realistically speaking, I think there are moments when it would be impossible to shoot an incoming missile down, as it will be up to North Korea as to where and at what time they fire it.

If they shoot it at dawn, it would be too early for the Japanese government to make decisions, and if the weather was bad on top of it, it would be even harder to detect.

What I am saying is that if an ICBM is shot at close range, Japan could suffer the same fate as Israel did in the past. I believe this is one of the reasons why UFOs are now frequenting Japan. They are trying to tell us something.

The aftereffects of atomic bomb
2) The shape of war of the 21st century

It is projected that the wars of the 21st century will no longer be limited to dropping bombs or shooting missiles. This is another thing to be considered.

Most of the Earth's civilization today is largely dependent on electric waves. So, it is projected that the satellites will be the first targets rather than the nation's cities or its ships. Of course, satellites are not normally supposed to be carrying weapons, but a certain country may have done so and put the satellite into orbit.

In that case, it would be possible for the object that is circling the Earth as a satellite to destroy another country's satellite, or for a space-shuttle-like object to be launched from earth to destroy the satellites of other countries.

And when satellites are destroyed, what will happen? It will make the nation almost defenseless because in most cases, intercontinental ballistic missiles or Aegis-ships—ships that function to gather information, detect attacks, and fire back—rely heavily on satellites. This is one of the projections being made.

There are also various new types of bombs that are being developed. So, considerations are being made on if a missile that is fired from somewhere higher than an aircraft, such as from outside the Earth's atmosphere, can be intercepted. If an attack comes from an object orbiting the Earth when it arrives right above its target, can it be intercepted? I don't think the capability is there, but this is another thing people are worried about.

Destroying satellites can also affect systems on earth. Almost everything runs on electricity, so an electromagnetic interference or radio frequency interference would disable TVs, radios, and phones. Trains, buses, bullet trains, and maglev trains could all be rendered useless. Therefore, I think warfare by disrupting information networks or by network shutdowns is also likely.

This tactic could cause the instant loss of all combat capabilities by destroying any system running on electricity. It would have the same effect as shooting an animal with a tranquilizer dart. It would work like anesthesia. And the more modernized the nation is, the greater effect the tranquilizer will have.

It would not only disrupt transportation and communication systems but also cause the collapse of the financial system. Majority of the financial system is now based on electronic payments. If someone ever thinks to destroy the financial system completely, they could wipe out the personal finances of individuals and of a whole nation, steal them, or do many other things.

Therefore, the wars of the 21st century will be very tricky indeed. Imagine that a system was disabled the moment it detected a nuclear missile launch. No one will be able to figure out who launched the missile. This is the argument that is happening over the cyberattacks between Russia and the United States as well as China and the United States.

If China were to attack Taiwan, I believe they will start by paralyzing Taiwan's modern technology. Their main focus will be to knock out their air defense system. I think they will start by causing a system malfunction so that it won't work and cannot communicate. How they will proceed from there, I think they are discussing that right now.

4

The True Work of the Messiah
to Protect Peace on Earth

Have faith in the God of the Earth
to stop the evil of materialism and scientism

In this way, wars will take on an unusual appearance from now on. The development of science and technology will at the same time lean toward advancing and encouraging materialism as well as hailing the triumph of materialistic science. However, science and technology do not clearly outline what is good and what is evil. What ends up happening is that whatever is superior defeats the inferior. Among those who are equal in their level of science and technology, the ones who have the greater power to attack are those who are more aggressive, have a greater liking for evil, and are more sensitive at detecting others' evil.

People who believe in conventional religions could face severe hardships when a non-religious, materialistic, atheistic country that believes in science becomes the following: thinks nothing of evil and controls people's thoughts with ideas such as, "Good and evil don't exist" and "Winning is good, losing is evil"; makes their citizens believe "patriotism for their country is good, good is when their country wins, and evil is when their country loses" as well as suppresses free speech, controls the press, and censors information; restricts freedom of movement and freedom of occupation for foreigners; and becomes able to exist independently by itself.

Therefore, what I must say on "What the Messiah Should Say and Do Now" is the following: If Japan holds on to the idea that the world will be at peace as long as Japan keeps its claws clipped and defangs itself based on a self-reproaching, repentant view of history stemming from long-held, postwar values, then we are approaching the time when Japan can no longer ever protect its own peace or the world's peace. This is one point.

If there is something that could deter materialistic scientism, one would be to have faith in God who thinks about the entire Earth. When there is a group of people whose faith transcends ethnic groups and nations, it will prove to be a strong deterrent. This is certain.

The way I have spoken may have sounded too objective. Should the activity of Happy Science stop growing at the level we are now, far from its goal, then that is not the true work of the Messiah.

For example, when Happy Science started the Happiness Realization Party (HRP) in 2009, it was partly because North Korea had developed nuclear weapons and was test-firing missiles one after another. Also, in the same year it was founded, the Japanese Democratic Party won the election and produced three prime ministers. But their approach was largely a policy of appeasement, currying up to China to secure their own power.

After that, the Abe administration came to power. But their response never went above the practice runs such as the wartime or prewar times: when there is a sign that North Korea is about to launch a missile, sirens will go off with calls for an evacuation drill. So, a fundamental solution was never reached.

So, under such a situation, if a politician of a country that lacks morals, a conscience, or faith in God really puts forth certain ideas, then there can be no opposing arguments. These are ideas such as "Putting our nation's survival first, defeating other countries, or taking over them is good" and "Anyone who disagrees will have their speech and thoughts censored, controlled, and banned from all the papers, TV, social media, everything. If they use it, they will be arrested."

People will only make speeches in favor of it. So, the approval rate would of course be close to 100 percent, although there might be some who keep their silence or abstain from casting their vote.

We will have to fight against this, so I believe correcting the postwar values is very important.

Japan's thoughtlessness from postwar reproaches and its approaching threat

I founded the HRP in 2009 because, in addition to North Korea's missiles, I saw what China was serious about doing. I saw its ambition to bring Japan under its control, drive back U.S. hegemony, make the seas as far as Hawaii its own, and bring Australia and Southeast Asian countries as well as a part of Africa and Europe into its sphere of control. There was a need for a political party that could speak up clearly, so I founded the HRP and began our activities.

But the Japanese media's intellectual level was not sufficiently high yet. Japanese scholars' intellectual level was also still at the level of reproaching themselves for the past war. Politicians considered "conscientious" are all left-wing liberals or human rights activists who only say, "Let's reflect on the bad things the Japanese military did," "We will never go to war again," or at rallies in Hiroshima, "May we never repeat the tragedy brought about by militarism ever again." But these are not solutions at all.

History teaches us that when a powerful nation appears, it will really annihilate nations. Whether it was Greece in the past or Israel, the Jewish kingdom before that, they really were destroyed, colonized, or enslaved.

This also happened in the Middle Ages. An empire called Yuan (Mongol) advanced all the way into Europe, occupied the Korean Peninsula, and then pushed into Japan. Japan fought back twice and protected the country in the Kamakura period. This is why Japan exists today.

It happened again during the Meiji restoration. China was being colonized by the western powers, so Japan rushed to open the country to the outside world. Many aspiring warriors, or "small messiahs," emerged, modernizing Japan to place it among the five most powerful countries in the world. In a way, this also served to protect the country.

However, a period of thoughtlessness has occurred since Japan's defeat in World War II and continues today. China celebrated the 100th anniversary of the CCP, but Japan has no power to stop it.

The Japanese Communist Party claims that they are different from the CCP. They often speak about opposing the CCP, but I do not know what they are really thinking. They are probably trying to keep their distance, perhaps afraid that if they align themselves completely with the CCP, they will have to abolish Japan's imperial system, and if they say so, they will not win in Japan's elections.

5

Why Is Communism Dangerous in the Eyes of the God of the Earth?

The dangers of communism
1) Affirmation of violence will provoke mass murder

I have spoken on communism before. In the late 1800s, Marx wrote *Capital* (*Das Kapital*). *The Communist Manifesto* was already published in the mid-1800s. But by the time of his death, only a few of his books were in circulation and he had only a few followers.

There were some socialist groups that began to use Marxism. As Marx himself said during his lifetime, "Marx and Marxism are different;" his theory had started being used differently, as a force to criticize the existing powers.

It really is a bit surprising that Marx, who died as a completely powerless and uninfluential figure, would become such a powerful figure a hundred years later.

But here is what I would like to state in short:

A communist society where "Everyone is equal" sounds like a good society. And in terms of human rights, it can be a force to break down the idea of keeping people in the class and status system they are born into. But one of the dangers of communism is that it affirms violent revolution.

Communism says, "Revolution is made by violence." So, wherever there has been a communist revolution, there have been mass killings. In fact, communism starts with genocide. And when someone rises to power through mass murder and revolution, this is how they will respond to any opposition or foreign power that tries to overthrow them to maintain their power.

So, a country that considers a revolution to be good will tend to think, "There is nothing sinful about mass murder against people who want to overthrow the regime that accomplished the revolution. It is justice. It is to protect the well-being of the people. And it is also to protect the patriots."

Certainly, countries have often been formed through unification by armed force or by seizing other lands, but it is dangerous to always have that way of thinking. They will eventually have to produce a set of values for coexistence at some point.

The dangers of communism
2) The spirit of hard work and capitalism is lost

I will talk about another danger.

This also arises out of basic human rights, but when you give people freedom, the freedom to strive freely, some will be hard-working and some will be lazy. Then, stark differences will arise. Those differences will become apparent in a generation or even as quickly as in one year or three years.

The question is, "What would happen if, no matter how large the difference becomes, a 'big government' always grinds down the disparity to make everyone the same?" The very spirit of diligent hard work would be lost.

The spirit of diligent hard work is what makes the spirit of capitalism. That is the "cycle of goodness" that involves holding your aspiration in the right direction, working hard, saving, and then growing your savings into greater capital, which will generate even larger investments that will enable you to carry out larger projects. Gradually, the society and the nation will become more prosperous. This is the spirit of capitalism.

But if a way of thinking that denies the accumulation of wealth is all there is—the thinking that "Once you have saved up money, it will be taken away from you through taxes or fines or by throwing you in jail so that your wealth can be redistributed to everyone equally"—then no one will be willing to work. Instead, the idea that "those who make money are evil" will emerge. This is contrary to the healthy spirit of capitalism.

And what will happen in the end? If the spirit of capitalism is destroyed but the state power wants to spend money, then fake money with no credible backing will be generated in various forms.

This is already in use. Starting with Bitcoin, many such virtual currencies are being created at the national level, but how it will turn out to be in the end is unclear.

For example, assets of a certain corporation that they had kept in cyberspace can disappear overnight because of a newly created law or regulation.

Recently, as we saw in Hong Kong, a newspaper company was prevented from accessing its funds to print its paper because the government froze its assets by national decree. The company, no longer able to pay its employees or even buy paper and ink, was forced to shut down, all while the world watched.

Not only was it the government that froze its assets, but it is also said that out of fear of the authorities, even banks and other institutions voluntarily froze assets, including those of the general public. I think it is quite possible that trust in finance and financial assets will eventually become a mirage too.

What will happen when this combines with Marxism? It will be possible to say, "All the money you possibly need could be created virtually. When those in power create virtual money, how much a working person saved, or how much internal funds a business has accumulated, will be completely meaningless."

Add military force to this and we will see the beginning of an age much like the reptilian (reptile-like space people) world of primitive times.

The dangers of communism
3) Faithlessness will give rise to tyrants

To explain why communism is not good, I talked about the problem of violent revolutions. I also said that communism destroys the real development of society or the development with credibility because it neither recognizes the spirit of capitalism as a cycle of goodness nor recognizes the freedom and fruits of hard work.

But the biggest problem must be the absence of faith. If you don't have faith, you would cease to be conscious of how God or Buddha sees you; so it is a way of thinking that inevitably allows whoever holds power on this earth to become a "living god." Regardless of how they think or whether they have the true support of the people or not, any person who holds the greatest authority on earth will be the "god" on earth.

This means that in China, for example, someone like the tyrant of ancient times will be able to call themselves a god. Under the rule of someone like that, no matter how many elections are held formally, the results couldn't be trusted. It could also expose who voted for whom. If you are found to have voted against the authority, you will be eliminated as a citizen. Elections would then become a very dangerous device.

6

The Modern Messiah's Message on What Humankind Must Do Now

From the standpoint of 2100, protect Hong Kong and Taiwan

Based on everything I have said so far, I must say that there is a movement to export the spirit of communism to uniformly manage the world. China is at the center of this, and North Korea is effectively doing the same.

In response, countries such as the United States, the United Kingdom, Germany, France, Australia, Taiwan, and Canada are showing their determination to prevent this. Alas, because their leaders are so weak, they don't make decisions or take necessary action and therefore settle on the policy of appeasing China as they are unable to deter it.

Australia, which only has a population of 20 million, used to adopt pro-China policies. But it now sees through China's ambition and has switched gears. China is imposing tariffs on imports from Australia to make the country suffer, but Australia is resisting the pressure and standing up to them.

Japan, on the other hand, is trying to eke out an existence by being like a bat—neither bird nor animal. However, when it comes to decisions that need to be made decisively, a spade must be called a spade; what must be said must be said. Japan must make a judgment and decide, "This is good, but this is evil" or "This should be stopped."

Therefore, thinking about what we must do today from the standpoint of 2100, we must "Protect Hong Kong." If, for example, the city of Hong Kong suffers devastating damage but the world simply watches, allows China to do what it pleases without any backlash, and lets it escalate, then the world would have overlooked a point at which it needed to have stepped in.

Second, with the same momentum as with Hong Kong, Beijing is also trying to take over Taiwan. Taiwan is a different country from China, but China asserts that Taiwan falls under its "one country, one system principle" (which they falsely claim to be "one country, two systems principle"). Here too, should the world think, "Better to let China take Taiwan than to risk a nuclear war" or "What does it matter if it's just Taiwanese pineapples that stop coming in?" then the result will inevitably be the same as when Hitler took over the neighboring countries one by one during World War II.

China is also saying that the Philippines and Japan's Senkaku Islands and Okinawa are its "core interests." Claiming that the Spratly Islands and the Paracel Islands are also their "core interests," they have built artificial islands on what were just reefs, turning them into their territory and building military bases on top of them. Other countries have not been able to do anything about it, so it will only be a matter of time before China comes for areas such as the Senkaku Islands and Okinawa, insisting they were "originally a part of the Chinese cultural sphere."

A part of this is certainly a question of at what point you step in to put a stop to this. But essentially, we must change our way of thinking.

The next thing to expect after
the Chinese biological weapon of novel coronavirus

The founding of HRP in 2009 has had such great historical significance. But Japan's mass media, political parties, government, scholars, cultural leaders, and the masses who receive their information from them chose to ignore it because they held the belief that "combining religion with politics is evil" and were more interested in keeping things the way they are. This amounts to a great sin. This is why UFOs are appearing. It is the second wave. In place of the black warships of the U.S. Navy that arrived off the coast of Shinagawa in the Edo period, UFOs are appearing today to wake Japan up.

The appearance of the next thing will follow later, but if Japan holds on to the way it has been living even while other countries are now waking up and feeling the threat, Japan must know that it is committing a very grave mistake.

Also, I don't know how history will be written about this in the future, but the COVID-19 (novel coronavirus infection) outbreak in 2019 has infected hundreds of millions of people around the world, has killed millions, and is still spreading.

Happy Science has repeatedly pointed out that the viruses are Chinese biological weapons. Even so, this opinion has probably not become mainstream yet. But if this too is overlooked because the world continues to appease China by saying, "The virus occurred naturally," it leaves the door open for China to use the next thing. In other words, China knows it cannot win a nuclear war yet, so they are likely to have waged a war with something else.

Spiritual Reading of Novel Coronavirus Infection Originated in China (Tokyo: HS Press, 2020)

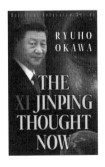

The Xi Jinping Thought Now (Tokyo: HS Press, 2021)

We must not stand by and let the righteous perish

In any case, we must not stand by and let the righteous perish. This is the direction in which the modern-day Messiah should speak and do the activities. This is the direction in which the Messiah should give guidelines for action and provide information, so that the world will take action.

Today, the spread of the coronavirus infection in the world has made it difficult to travel freely from one country to another, but we should be well aware of what is underway right now.

Many movies in the second half of the 20th century depicted the utter finality a thermonuclear war would bring. But in the case of a biological weapon or a chemical weapon, you may not be aware of its usage right away.

That is why we need to establish universal values now and review what the different academic fields and occupational fields are doing from the standpoint of the values that come from the Supreme God and Buddha.

Japan has suffered, at least politically, the first round of defeat with the failure of the HRP to join the government after more than 10 years of activity. But if we can foresee future defeats, there are some things that have to be changed now.

Envision how humanity must be like from the eyes of the God of the Earth

I have spoken in various ways about how Japan and the world should be. It is of course important to follow the news or read newspapers to know what is happening in the world, and it is okay to have some knowledge of such miscellaneous day-to-day information or to get your information from your smartphone or cellphone, but chances are that they do not contain much information coming from Ryuho Okawa. Very little of it is likely communicated on TV, in the newspapers, and on your smartphones and cellphones.

That is why I believe we must absolutely deliver to every part of the world Happy Science's ultimate, brief judgments on good and evil and the guidelines on the direction of how things should be.

This is what we must aim for and make efforts toward. By making efforts, we can achieve what the old saying says, "A journey of a thousand miles begins with a single step." If we don't move forward step by step, nothing will progress.

Please do not give up.

Please deny the idea of maintaining the status quo.

Please know that we cannot be just one of the religions in Japan, least of all, a corporation.

Please do not take pleasure in the fall of the good and the rise of the evil.

Please do not think that only science and technology, legal systems, and political systems created by human beings in this world are precious.

Since Kant, academic disciplines have not treated what is not fit for academic research as their subjects. This very attitude excludes matters of the unknown and matters of faith from the academic world, removing their citizenship. I would like you to know this.

Also, when liberalism goes too far, it limits itself to the protection of human rights in this world alone. But we must envision how humanity must be like from the eyes of God.

Even if it's a "small battle," if it is symbolic, fight strongly and win

Look at the tragedy of Sodom and Gomorrah in the Old Testament and know that God does not forgive when humankind becomes degenerate. And against those who strengthen the hands of evildoers and cut down those who do good, just as a boy named David once defeated a three-meter-tall giant named Goliath with just stone and rope—a simple weapon of stones tied to the ends of a cord—do not be fearful of the physical size but do what is just.

It is incredible that a shepherd boy fought a three-meter-tall giant and won.

Goliath said, "Anyone who can defeat me, come out! Have a one-on-one battle with me." Then a shepherd boy came forward. Because he was an expert at throwing stones with a rope tied to them, he threw them at the giant and brought him down by crushing his eye. This really happened.

Even a small act such as this led to "the act of the Messiah," saving the kingdom of Israel. Later, David became known as a great king.

The target may seem small. But if that small battle is a symbolic one, then winning it will render a great impact later on. Rather than trying to win on all fronts, please think again with a worldly, practical mind about securing small but symbolic victories and push forward with it.

Furthermore, regarding things that human beings on earth cannot fully address, messages will come down from the universe. Although it would be easy to laugh and ridicule them, please pass them on to the world as the truth and as a complement to the words of the Messiah of the Earth, or use them as words to enlighten the Japanese people.

The future I envision is that as of 2100,
The British–American values or Japanese values will
Abolish racial discrimination
And will still be producing ideas that are closer to God's
To conduct politics, create the economy, and create a culture
In a way that is not associated with military dominance.

This is the state of the world I wish will continue,
So resolutely resist when you can resist any movement
That takes the world in the opposite direction.

Should Japan get taken over
Or threatened with nuclear weapons by a certain country,
The Japanese people's faith will be shut down.
Free speech and free press,
Which are founded on freedom of religion, will disappear.
Academic freedom will go, too,
And so will freedom of conscience.
The judicial courts will become meaningless
Because the decision would already be clear from the beginning.
This will cause everything that humankind
Had acquired as wisdom in the modern era
To go to waste.
We must therefore continue this fight.

The Teachings of Messiah

The Battle to Change the Values with Words of God

1

The Difficulty of Acknowledging the Messiah, the One Chosen by God

I chose a bold title for this chapter, "The Teachings of Messiah." This will be less of an organized talk, but I would be happy if I could talk to you about what I am feeling and thinking along the lines of what the teachings of a Messiah are, what is needed now, and what is going to be needed in the future.

Today, things are not like the past. It has become very difficult for a messianic being to be acknowledged by the world. The word Messiah might not sound familiar to Japanese people, but Messiah is, in other words, savior. People often associate a savior with someone who liberates people from suffering and hardships, guides them, and creates a new age. You may imagine these to be a savior's work. The word Messiah also has the same meaning, but the original meaning of Messiah is "the one who has been anointed on the head." Anointed by whom? By God. So, it is God who anoints a Messiah.

In Japan, a similar Buddhist custom called *kanjo* exists where water is poured on people's heads so that they are purified. In Buddhism, such a ritual is conducted when appointing monks to higher positions. It aligns with the idea of ancient Judaism that says, "A Messiah is the one who has been anointed by God."

And because this person is chosen by God, we do not know how he or she could appear, as the appearance will be irrespective of status, position, age, or gender. People will later on, or in the same age while the person is still alive, sense that he or she is the one chosen by God.

However, modern civilization has a huge population; nearly eight billion people live on Earth. Some countries are operated under a democratic system, whereas others have a totalitarian regime. For this reason, the process of finding the chosen one, having him revered, having his words accepted as God's words, and realizing these words on earth is extremely difficult.

This is partly because modern people have distanced themselves from spiritual beings or inspiration. In this sense, we can say that people have become less spiritual. Another reason is that as the population increases, people have created many systems to enable a lot of people to live together in an orderly manner. So, the chosen one will need to break through these barrier-like systems first before being able to stand in the position of guiding people, and this is not easy to do.

A Messiah usually appears when there is a major clash of values on earth. Such a day and age are usually when many people do not understand what is right and what is wrong and cannot differentiate good from bad. In general, the thoughts and opinions that the majority have in common will often become reality. So there is no need for the chosen one to appear to make it happen. When a Messiah appears, in most cases, his work will be to present and uphold the thoughts and ideas that have never been voiced before— or thoughts and ideas that are supported by only a small number of people—to create a great surge of movement by gaining supporters, and to overturn and correct the public opinion or value systems of the age.

So, a Messiah is often a minority who is trying to correct the value systems while confronting the huge existing power. That is why his work can often end up being unfulfilled in this world.

In addition, occupations have become very specialized and specific in this age, leaving many doors open, so there are hardly any jobs that can put people in very advantageous positions. This makes things even more difficult.

What job could the one who saves the world be doing if he appears in this modern age? This is a very difficult question. It was simple in the olden times, as it was obviously a religious leader. But could a Buddhist monk or Christian priest or pastor of today carry out the work of a Messiah? I believe it will be very difficult.

Monks, priests, and pastors usually belong to large organizations with established hierarchies. Under these circumstances, a Messiah may try to make himself stand out by demonstrating a unique ability that others do not have. For example, he may have a special psychic power or might be able to save people by healing their illnesses. But in the modern age, these abilities alone are not enough for the individual to be acknowledged as the one who has been chosen by God.

2

The Fight over the Values in History: Messiah vs. Worldly Authority

It is not easy to fight authority with an army using words and thoughts alone

Based on school education and information from mass media, the one chosen by God will often be labeled as a swindler or imposter and be buried into obscurity. If they succeed in getting many followers and support, they will then be regarded as dangerous individuals by the authorities and be oppressed by police or military forces. Not many leaders can win against the forces that use guns, tanks, and fighter jets in these times.

Now that the world has become large and complicated, many leaders are born with a mission on a national level rather than a global level. Gandhi and Martin Luther King Jr. are some examples of leaders who achieved their goals by sticking to non-violence and non-resistance, but these are rare exceptions. In most cases, non-violent and non-resistant leaders will most likely end up being oppressed by the armed police or military forces. In this way, it is not easy to make people believe and follow with words and thoughts alone.

A few years ago, I conducted a spiritual reading on the leader of the Taiping Rebellion (Hong Xiuquan) that occurred in China in the 1850s during the Qing Dynasty. It is said that about 50 million people were killed in the rebellion. So, even though a leader who appeared to be a savior rose and led the rebellion, the Qing Dynasty—which would eventually be destroyed—was able to crack down on the rebellion with its authoritative power and kill 50 million people.

In Chinese history, there have been many incidents in which tens of millions of people were killed. Emperor Wu[2] of Han is also famous in Chinese history, but it is said that the population halved during his reign. In this way, a political leader who possesses military forces is very powerful.

Usually, religious ideas are what give rise to a revolution. At that time, the government not only oppresses it using military forces but also tends to force certain ways of thinking—or ideologies—on the people so they can be easily controlled. For example, Confucians were persecuted during the reign of the First Emperor of Qin[3] but during the reign of Emperor Wu of Han, the government officially adopted Confucianism. Even so, seeing that the population reduced to half, means that there were food shortages, and because there was not enough food to eat, many people were killed. The government took advantage of Confucianism to make the people submissive and prevent any rebellion from arising.

The current Beijing government is doing the same; it has opened the Confucius Institutes disguised as Chinese language schools around the world and is gradually brainwashing people. The world is now cautious of these, and investigation has started in some countries. Japan has also started investigating the Confucius Institutes that operate inside various universities.

Like so, the government often puts up an ideology that is convenient for it to use to control its people and prevent uprisings. It uses that as a substitute for religious belief.

Preventing uprisings was crucial for Japan's Tokugawa Shogunate, as well. It used military forces to suppress Christians and to oppress the Shimabara Rebellion[4]. But it was more important for the Shogunate to nip any potential rebellion in the bud. So, it created political and economic systems that enabled it to do so and forced philosophy based on Confucianism onto people to make them stay loyal to the superior. It made sure people would learn the ways of masters and servants and controlled the people in this way. Thus, a philosophy that can be used for social reform may sometimes be abused by those in power.

What is more, mass media has huge power in the modern democratic society. There are many kinds of mass media—newspapers, TV stations, radio programs, and recently the Internet—but there are no clear leaders among them. They are usually anonymous powers, and these anonymous powers choose or discard specific people.

Even if you try to tell people the words and the Will of God via mass media or your own "mini media," they will only go viral and capture many people's hearts when people have a good level of capability and a certain degree of openness. If not, it can sometimes have a negative impact. In some cases, people are more inclined to accept the thoughts of the devil.

The government can control its people
by abusing the system

Materialism-based science may seem to have a neutral stance, as it can work positively or negatively depending on the situation. But if people are more focused on things from a materialistic point of view, they will lose sight of their minds and live without thinking about their souls.

Of course, materialism is sometimes necessary to improve life on earth. For example, there was an age of food shortages, an age of famine, and an age when epidemics such as smallpox or the black plague broke out. In such an age, installing a sewerage system and promoting disinfection were necessary, as many people's lives can be lost owing to bad sanitary conditions. Therefore, materialistic efforts cannot be altogether denied. The difficulty is on how to use the materialistic approaches wisely.

Some Chinese classics explain the reason for the outbreak of war as follows: "The population increases, but the amount of food does not. So, when the population grows, people will start to kill each other to secure their food. The strong will destroy the weak and try to reduce the number of people to obtain food for themselves. This is the primary cause of war."

In a sense, this is true. As you can see from the 20th century, whenever there is less food and energy, industries cannot be sustained. When people have difficulty gaining their daily food, a war often breaks out. In the primitive stage, a poor ratio of food to the population can be a real problem that triggers a war.

In the next stage, when a country gets stronger, it can have a stronger desire just like a person does. A leader with a strong intention to seize power will emerge and try to control others. Thomas Hobbes used the words Leviathan— the master of the sea—and Behemoth—the ruler of the land—to explain sovereignty. Indeed, a leader with a strong will to gain power can go on a rampage like a huge monster and oppress his people or neighboring countries and try to make them obey him.

For this reason, the kind of systems that are created really does not matter because those in power can abuse them. For example, some centuries ago, the government was able to completely suppress the people using the tax system. Salt, for instance, is one of the necessities of life, so depending on how much tax the government decides to impose on salt, it can control its people.

The government can also tax rice. Conventionally, tax has been imposed on rice in Japan. Ever since Hideyoshi Toyotomi[5] conducted the nationwide land survey, people were taxed based on how much rice they could reap from their land. There was such a time. So, the government controls the people by manipulating the circulation or the pricing of the necessities of life or by imposing taxes on them; a huge power can emerge there.

• *The fight over values* 1) Religious wars in Japan

Also, a fight over value systems can truly take place. For example, conflicts similar to religious wars occurred many times in Japan. In the age of Prince Shotoku[6], there was a clash between the people who revered traditional Japanese gods and the people who considered Buddhism, which had come from India via China, as more advanced and superior. A fight then occurred between the Soga and Mononobe clans.

In the Kamakura period too, when many new religious groups arose, the fight over value systems occurred even between the different schools of Buddhism. For example, the Nichiren school of Buddhism was founded after the rise of the schools that teach chanting, which were started by monks such as Honen and Shinran.

When Honen and Shinran founded the chanting schools, they attracted many believers, even the court ladies of the emperor, so they were persecuted and exiled to a distant land. But by the time Nichiren appeared, the chanting schools were widely spread after decades of activities. When the newly arisen Nichiren criticized the preceding chanting schools, these schools went to oppress the Nichiren school with the support of samurai warriors.

The monks of the Nichiren school also armed themselves and stored Japanese halberds, bows, and arrows in their temples. In the well-known persecution in Komatsubara, the samurai who believed in the chanting schools assaulted the monks of the Nichiren school, injuring Nichiren and killing some of his disciples.

Nichiren also predicted the Mongol invasion attempts against Japan. He believed that a country that is not based on the right Buddhist teachings would invite a foreign invasion, so he urged the government to uphold the right teachings to stop the invasion from abroad. But he was arrested instead and was about to be beheaded at Yuigahama Beach in Kamakura. He was then exiled to Sado Island. After the Mongolians truly came to invade Japan, Nichiren had his sentence reduced, and he retreated to Mt. Minobu. In the end, Nichiren did not succeed in spreading his teachings throughout the country; considering the difference in the population then and now, the number of his followers back then would have only been several hundred in the modern context.

It is very difficult to win against those in power. It is also difficult to win against the preceding forces. If you set forth a philosophy that conflicts with that of the preceding forces who already have considerable power, you can be persecuted. This has happened many times.

• *The fight over values* 2) Distrust in Christianity and the persecution of Christians

When Jesus Christ appeared, thousands of people followed him and listened to his sermons. He was first expected to be the Messiah people had been waiting for. But in the context of Judaism, the Messiah should not only be a religious leader but also be a political leader. A Messiah must convey the words of God and, at the same time, under the banner of God, be able to stand against any invasion and colonization from other countries in realpolitik.

During the time of Jesus, the Pharisees and the Zealots were involved in political movements, and they had expected Jesus to work as an agitator and incite the mob to put up a fight against the Romans and expel them. But Jesus said, "Give therefore to the emperor the things that are the emperor's and to God the things that are God's." Because the coins in those times had the face of Caesar, Jesus said that they should be returned to Caesar.

Jesus divided things based on two values—things that belong to God and things that belong to the emperor on earth. On hearing this, people were disappointed and thought that Jesus would not be able to win against earthly powers. This is clearly written in the Bible.

The Bible also has the description of the scene where thousands of people were shocked to hear some of Jesus' sermons and left him. For example, the Eucharist is now a common practice in Christianity, and the attendants eat a thin, cracker-like piece of bread and drink wine. This practice comes from the metaphor Jesus had used. Jesus broke bread and gave it to his disciples, and he drank wine during his last supper. Jesus likened the bread to his body and wine to his blood and said something like, "Those who eat my flesh and drink my blood will be saved." On hearing such sermons, many of his believers were said to have felt disappointed and deserted him.

In fact, people could not understand what Jesus meant. His metaphor is not very beautiful either. Eating his body and drinking his blood sounds like something Dracula would do, and it is spooky; it was more than a thousand and a few hundred years before Count Dracula appeared. If you read the Bible thoroughly, you can see that many people left, for they couldn't understand the metaphor. In the end, only his 12 apostles and a handful of his followers remained with him.

People had expected Jesus to be a political revolutionary, but they lost the hope they had in Jesus. At the same time, they found Jesus' teachings weird—like the reptilians' philosophy—and could not really understand what he was trying to say. They had expected his teachings to be more attractive and to spread widely if he truly was the one sent by God.

In the end, Jesus was crucified and the cross became the symbol of Christianity. This is unbelievable. In Japan, it would be the same as wearing the pendant of a tombstone. So, Christianity is quite a peculiar religion. It is probably because they aimed to overturn the values of this world that they used those various symbols.

Jesus was only able to carry out his missionary work for three years when he was alive. But many capable disciples appeared in later generations, and Christianity gradually gained power.

Christianity spread into the Roman Empire as well. In the beginning, Christians were treated as bad people. They carried out activities underground. They were believed to always plot revenge and do bad things because they bore grudges against the Roman Empire. So, whenever a bad incident happened, they were accused.

It is a typical way for political leaders to create their enemies and persecute them to unite the country. Just like how Hitler tried to empower himself by persecuting the Jews, the Roman Empire persecuted Christians. For example, when the great fire occurred in Rome and much of the city was destroyed under Emperor Nero, Christians were held accountable and suffered great oppression.

More than 300 years after that, however, the tables turned and those who were persecuted became the persecutors. There is such an irony of fate, and this is the difficult part. This happens due to the limitations of human recognition. When it comes to things that cannot be seen with the eyes, people cannot understand what is true and cannot tell whether something comes from God or the devil.

Jesus also performed miracles and cured people of their illnesses. Many people saw these as the work of God but some did not. There are such people in every age.

When Jesus cured an illness, he said, "See that you tell no one," and commanded people not to tell anyone in the family or elsewhere. But people could not hold back and told others that they regained their sight or their ability to rise and walk again. They widely spread the news, and this also raised doubt in people who were suspicious of Jesus' activities and people with vested interests. These people called Jesus a swindler or imposter; some even said it was the work of the devil.

To them, Jesus refuted, "How can Satan cast out Satan?" He said, "Every house divided against itself will not stand." By this, he meant, "If Satan drives out the evil spirits that try to control humans and make them ill, hell will be like a divided house; things will not go well there. There is no way Satan does such a thing in his realm." However, I feel this logic is not convincing enough.

If people on earth are excessively influenced by spirits, it would be very difficult for them to work properly, have a family, and lead a decent life without going insane. That is why people are usually unable to see any spiritual beings or hear their words. It's how they were made to be. If people can see spiritual beings and hear their voices, they will most likely go insane.

Some people have spiritual abilities or are strongly sensitive to spiritual matters, but it takes a lot of effort for them to live a normal life among ordinary people and work comfortably with others. Suppose a person says to you, "I can see a ghost in front of me," "I just heard the voice of the devil," or "An angel has come down to me and given me such messages." It would be hard to work with such a person in a normal office.

Then, will he or she be able to work in churches? Churches also have a clear hierarchy. If the person at the top—such as the pope—can heal people's illnesses, it may be a good thing; the number of Catholic believers might increase. But what if a person of a lower rank can heal people's illnesses or exorcise evil spirits? If his work is highly recognized, the hierarchy of the church—or the pyramid of value—will be overturned, so usually, his work is not approved or recognized. That is why miracles hardly occur even in the circle of religion.

Some conflicting values are wiped out by the victors in history

Sometimes the value judgment will become clear with time, but many values are buried into obscurity and disappear without being recognized. This is true with wars. Most wars occur due to the clash of values, but because history is usually written by victors, it is difficult to tell where justice truly lies.

According to the Chinese philosophy of revolution, Tiandi, the Emperor of Heaven, sends a ruler into this world and orders him to govern the people, but if he becomes an evil ruler, a revolution will happen and a new dynasty will be built. So, in Chinese history, a dynasty lasted no more than 400 years. There is such a philosophy of revolution in China.

At present, China is based on a one-party system and is ruled by the Communist Party. The current Communist Party also uses this philosophy of revolution to its advantage. To claim that the ruler is supported by heaven's will, they announce good statistics to show how significantly people's lives have improved. They also one-sidedly announce how much their country, which used to be under the great threat of foreign attack, has developed and become stronger. However, under their system, Mao Zedong and other lifelong leader-like people have become "living gods with real power."

In fact, according to my spiritual research, most of such Chinese leaders of the past are now in hell. I feel reluctant to say this, but many post-revolution leaders of the Soviet Union—current Russia—have also gone to hell. It seems that a new bill was passed in Russia to condemn those who denounce the past Soviet leaders, so it is difficult to say such a thing now. It is similar to North Korea, but apparently, Russia can now punish those who criticize or denounce their founding fathers as political criminals.

Under such a situation, how can we know what is right? There is the issue of existing religions having their own values. There is also the question of what the source of authority in this secular world is. And there is the strong influence of mass media, which has great power in a democratic society. Factors such as these make it extremely difficult for people to perceive what the modern Messiah is like.

3

Modern Groups of People that Confuse the Teachings of Messiah

Those who praise and take advantage of the climate activist Ms. Greta

The other day, I watched a TV special featuring the year-long activity of a Swedish girl Ms. Greta, who is now 18 years old. I think it was a program produced by the BBC, and whose rights to air were bought by a Japanese TV station. It closely covered how a teenage girl continues her activities as she challenges world leaders.

Ms. Greta was a high school student when she first started her activities. She decided to not attend school and went on a strike. The news of her strike spread widely through the Internet, and many people followed suit in different countries.

She is hostile toward those who she thinks are causing global warming and accuses adults for "stealing" children's future. Based on the belief that global warming must be stopped, she condemns politicians, business leaders, industrialists, and others who are responsible for global warming. Her point is that justice lies in science, and she says something like, "This is what science teaches. You must listen to the science."

Someone who refuses to go to school and is on strike—someone who does not study—talks of science. When Mr. Trump was the U.S. president, he apparently confronted her and told her to go to school and study. He suggested she go back to high school and go on to study in college. As an adult, what he said is a matter of course.

In fact, Ms. Greta has at large been taken advantage of as a symbol. She has been used as a symbolic analyst. She is a child—a girl—so adults find it hard to attack her. Mass media favors this kind of person. Mass media likes to portray the weak as superior and strong and attack the strong to drag them down. This is the basic principle of mass media. So, Ms. Greta was easily taken advantage of. The TV program portrayed Ms. Greta to be a modern Joan of Arc or savior fighting against global warming.

We were curious to know her true nature and conducted spiritual research on her, which was published as a book (refer to *On Carbon footprints reducing - Why Greta gets angry?*). In the spiritual interview, a spirit that called itself Noah who

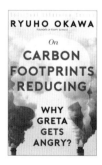

On Carbon footprints reducing - Why Greta gets angry? (Tokyo: HS Press, 2020)

survived the Great Flood appeared first. But the spirit was obviously different from the Noah of the story of Noah's Arc, whom we had previously conducted spiritual research on. Although the spirit called itself Noah, it was actually a different kind of spirit that instigates fear by warning against a doomsday crisis. Such a spirit was found to be possessing Ms. Greta. What is more, it has become clear that the spirit of Lenin, one of the key figures of the Russian Revolution, was also active behind the scenes to influence her.

In addition, it is known that Ms. Greta receives financial support from organizations that have close ties with the Beijing government. By putting these pieces of information together, we can see that there is a grand plan to destroy the prosperity of developed nations of the Western Bloc and that she is taken in and used to help realize this.

Some industries have indeed shifted direction to counter global warming and reduce the amount of CO_2 emissions, and new businesses have been created. But Ms. Greta does not have a clear idea about the world economy, economic recession, or the issues of unemployment or food shortages. She is not a politician and does not understand the economy or business management either.

When Mr. Trump was in office, he strived to revive the Rust Belt, the areas with many white residents, which used to produce coal or manufacture cars but have now become poor. He tried hard to bring back jobs there. To Ms. Greta, those people, too, probably seem evil. But she needs to know that the world is more complicated than she imagines.

Climate scientists consider various hypotheses, such as "What would happen if the average temperature on Earth rises by 2°C or 1.5°C?" and make calculations in many ways. But this is similar to the current situation where scholars of infectious diseases intervene in political decisions in Japan and the world. These scholars voice their opinions based only on the study of infectious diseases and virology and cannot take responsibility for what will happen if their suggestions are implemented. If you see things from a single perspective, through a tiny hole, you will end up overlooking other aspects.

Sometimes you can be taken advantage of by some foreign groups, so you need to be careful.

We need wisdom to see through secret plots set by evil countries

Scientists are threatening people by insisting that global warming will bring about the same phenomenon as in the story of Noah's Arc and will submerge earth. According to their theory, Earth receives energy from the sun and radiates it back into space, keeping Earth's temperature moderately low, but if CO_2 is highly concentrated in the upper atmosphere, it will trap the heat and raise the temperature. They may well see this kind of phenomenon in experiments.

However, there is also another perspective. Even if CO_2 and other gases accumulate in the upper atmosphere, they will also block the sunlight from reaching the earth. Taking this into account, it is hard to say definite things.

What is more, in the long history of Earth, there were times when Earth was much, much hotter. There is no doubt that Earth was burning 4.6 billion years ago. It was an extremely hot ball of thick lava, which gradually cooled off. Parts of lava became rocks, then mountains, rivers, and oceans were formed, and living creatures were born hundreds of millions of years ago.

Happy Science knows that humans already existed when dinosaurs were still roaming the earth. The gigantic dinosaurs were able to survive in those times because the climate was warm, and the plants were thriving. Herbivorous dinosaurs grew large, and the carnivorous dinosaurs that fed on them and other big animals thrived as well. There were many large animals in an age when Earth was much warmer than it is now. Humans were also living in such an age. This is a fact.

Therefore, global warming does not mean the extinction of humanity. Rather, it has created an environment that allows plants, animals, and humans to be born and to live, so I do not think it is a life-threatening problem. Unless Earth is warm, it is difficult for many lives to be born and to grow. There are many big fish in warm oceans but not as many in cold waters. The same is true with plants. Farming is difficult in snow, but once the snow melts, it is possible to grow crops and vegetables. The number of animals will also increase.

From an overall perspective, humanity has repeated different experiences in its long history. So, our future will not be determined by the human calculation of the rise in temperature by 1.5°C, 2°C, or 4°C. Different factors are actually at work beyond the degree of temperature. For example, there are convection currents in Earth's mantle, where melting magma flows. So, global warming is not the only factor behind the rising and sinking of land. The movement of underground magma can also cause such phenomena.

It is said that 330 million years ago, in the age of Alpha, the continents of Africa, Europe, and Asia were all connected to form the Pangaea Continent. Alpha descended to the Pangaea Continent, so we cannot exactly say that Alpha was born in Africa, Europe, or Asia. As the theory of tectonic plates suggests, the continent then separated into different parts. But this had nothing to do with global warming.

The mass media only reports the images of melting sea ice or polar bears almost drowning, giving an impression that global warming is a huge problem.

But this is the media strategy that was used at the start of the Gulf War and the Iraq War as well. At the time of the Gulf War, the media reported the image of waterbirds covered in Iraqi oil and how seriously their lives were affected. They also reported on the testimony of a girl—who was later found to be the daughter of the then-Kuwaiti ambassador to the United States—about the disastrous situation of Kuwait, which provoked strong anger among the U.S. lawmakers. It is clear by now that the Gulf War and the Iraq War were planned wars.

Japanese people today are quite ignorant of world affairs, but many countries in the world aggressively plot various evil deeds to benefit themselves only. We must know this.

The coronavirus pandemic that broke out around December 2019 has already led to about 267 million infected cases and millions of deaths as I speak. The number of infections surpassed 49 million in the United States and 34 million in India, followed by Brazil. The major European countries and Russia also have 9-10 million cases, and the pandemic is spreading in Southeast Asia as well (as of December 7, 2021). Only China, which has 1.4 billion citizens, claims that it has succeeded in containing the virus at the initial stage and that the infections have not increased from 100,000 cases.

North Korea, on the other hand, announced that there have been no confirmed cases of coronavirus. Even though it has no coronavirus cases, some top officials were purged for failing to take necessary measures against coronavirus infection, which is quite strange.

In countries without fact-reporting media, those in power can make up any figures to declare during an official announcement. Other countries should not deal or negotiate with such countries seriously. We must bear this in mind.

The world is not full of good people only. The philosophy of Machiavelli—known as the father of modern political science—can be useful in a sense if you selectively use his wisdom. That is, "Some countries, or rather a president or a prime minister, may have evil thoughts." This is one thing that we may want to keep in mind.

4

The Teachings of Messiah Required in This Age

Communist countries block out the teachings of Messiah

In a nutshell, today's age is difficult; things do not go easily even if a Messiah is sent from heaven.

In our recent spiritual research, we found that John Lennon of The Beatles is a part of the soul of Jesus Christ. The spirit of John Lennon is helping us with creating music, so we now have a deeper connection with him.

The songs of The Beatles spread to hundreds of millions of people around the world. But how were they toward the end? In the beginning, the band was so popular for a few years that many fans fainted during their concert in a stadium; the police were mobilized, and ambulances were called into the stadium to treat the fainted. Apparently, the band members including John Lennon were sad to see this because they just wanted their fans to enjoy their music. I think they reached the limits of their activities. They reached their limits around the time they started holding concerts in stadiums.

After some years of activity, The Beatles disbanded. John Lennon married Yoko Ono and the couple had a child. For about five years, he was a househusband and spent his time raising his child. He did not carry out any musical activities during that time. After that, he decided to restart his activities as a solo artist and was planning to produce a new album.

On December 8, 1980, John Lennon was stopped by one of his fans when he was leaving his home at the Dakota Apartments. He was asked to sign a copy of his album, so he signed it. Five hours later, when he came back from the recording, he was met by the same man again in front of the house. John thought he was a mere fan of his, but the man held up a gun and fired at John five times, four of which hit him. I believe the man fired twice at his wife as well but none of them hit her.

When asked why he killed John Lennon, the man apparently said it was for "self-glory." Sadly, in a gun society like the United States, angels cannot spread their wings to block the gunfire even to protect someone like John Lennon. This is very sad. I have not conducted any spiritual research on the killer, so I am not sure if he was possessed by the devil.

I went to see the site where John was killed about one and a half years after the incident. As his contemporary, I barely crossed paths with him.

At the beginning of his activities, John Lennon sang songs that attracted young female fans and gained much popularity. But after immigrating to the United States, he protested the Vietnam War under the administrations of President Nixon and others, including the bombings of North Vietnam and the dropping of napalm bombs that killed many Vietnamese farmers. This is the symbol of rock music.

John started singing songs like "Power to the People." He had already seen through the evil character of China after Mao Zedong's revolution. He was so critical of the United States for bombing Vietnam that he was once ordered to leave the country. However, although he criticized the United States for their one-sided attack on Vietnam, he was also aware that China was wrong after Mao Zedong's revolution.

He thought he could change China if he could hold a concert at Tiananmen Square. He also thought that if The Beatles could hold a concert at the square of the Kremlin in the Soviet Union (now Russia), they could change the world. But the communist countries utterly shut them out. These countries blocked The Beatles because they were not sure of the philosophy behind their music. So, even if John wanted to go there to hold a concert, he could not. This shows that there were battles behind the scenes.

John Lennon wrote a song criticizing Mao Zedong and wanted to put it on the A-side of a single, but apparently, he was pressured into putting it in on the B-side. So, I am guessing that some people had secretly wanted to murder him for political reasons.

This is very sad; someone like John Lennon could only do so much in this world. Hong Xiuquan, the leader of the Taiping Rebellion in China, is said to be part of the soul of Zoroaster, but 50 million people were killed during the rebellion.

In Hong Kong, too, many activists have been arrested, and they feel their lives are in danger. It does not take the military to oppress them; the police are enough to arrest and torture them. When pro-democracy activists in Hong Kong are arrested as anti-government protesters, they are stripped naked, photographed, and sent to Beijing in sacks. The aim is to make them experience the feeling of helplessness out of humiliation, just like how rats are conditioned to eventually stop looking for food after experiencing electric shocks. The torture culture still exists today.

The Uyghurs in the Xinjiang Uyghur Autonomous Region and the members of Falun Gong that oppose the Beijing government also get caught. It is becoming clear that after they are caught, they are used for organ transplants. Although the dead do not speak, this seems to be true.

The official number of brain deaths, allowing organ donation, is no more than thousands of cases in China, so essentially China cannot provide more organs than that. But apparently, some organs are provided in a matter of 10 minutes in China now. They can provide a considerable number of organs. From this, it is estimated that these organs are taken from the criminals on death row, people of different races captured in the autonomous regions, and the believers of the religion Falun Gong, which is oppressed by the government. And these are conducted under the good name of "saving people's lives through medical means."

Such conduct will not stop unless the UN forces go into China. We must know that such things are occurring even now.

We also need to know that there are many nuclear test sites in East Turkestan with Uyghur residents, and many underground tests, ground tests, and explosion tests in the air were carried out in the past. The number of deaths caused by these nuclear tests is said to be hundreds of thousands. Many Uyghurs—more than the number of people who died in the atomic bombings of Hiroshima and Nagasaki—were killed because of the nuclear tests. China is such a country that can hide these facts as well.

In this age of confusing values,
what the Messiah must say to change the future

• Regarding dictatorial and totalitarian regimes and democratic and free nations

Now, at this point, we can still change our future.

I give simple messages so that people can understand them well. Some countries are under dictatorship and have a totalitarian regime that can oppress their people. Under such a regime, even if 80 percent of the people find something wrong, they cannot voice their opinions. These countries also develop nuclear weapons and have the ambition to invade other countries. So, it is important to stop the future that they are trying to create and block the dark clouds from casting over the world. And it is the people of the Western Bloc, who adopt many people's opinions, who must do so.

As for democratic nations, some elements make people corrupt and decadent. So, you need the will to control yourself. Free countries also have some elements that only work to corrupt people, so you need to be careful.

Freedom of corruption can produce devils. So, people who share Western values must have self-discipline, be responsible for society, and be responsible to make other people happy. If there are churches and you believe in

Christianity, for example, you must make your religious belief tangible and manifest it on earth.

• Advice for Muslim countries

There are problems in Muslim countries, too. All people are considered equal under Allah who cannot be seen, but in this idea lies the way of thinking that justifies poverty and prevents their societies from developing and prospering. I believe people must make efforts to change their societies into ones where each individual can find their own way, improve themselves, and enjoy prosperity through their own efforts.

People who believe in religion must also make efforts; we need to put soul into an empty-shell religion that only sticks to the formality. We also need to consider from the perspective of God and Buddha how science and technology should advance and be used for military purposes and how space technology should be used.

So, from a historical perspective, the role of a Messiah has become quite restricted.

• Regarding the system called "nation under the rule of law"

Another example is Nelson Mandela, who was born in South Africa and became a president. He is said to have devoted himself to activities for freeing black people and realizing equality between the black and the white. According to Happy Science spiritual research, his soul is one of the soul siblings of Moses (refer to *Nelson Mandela's Last Message to the World*).

But even he had spent 27 years in prison. This is very hard. For him to finally get out of prison and, even, to become a president was probably because the tide of the times had also changed. From the perspective of the heavenly plan, it was almost like he was walking a tightrope. There was no guarantee that Mandela could truly become a president and free the black people.

South Africa is another country that is suffering from the coronavirus pandemic. Poverty prevails, and many shopping malls have been looted; society is not safe now.

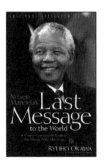

Nelson Mandela's Last Message to the World (Tokyo: HS Press, 2013)

When poverty prevails and riots occur, police and military forces will be mobilized. Depending on the situation, a military government can be formed after that. We can see many such patterns happening around the world. The military staged a coup d'état in Thailand, and the military government still prevails. The same is true with Myanmar.

If politicians fail to create enemies outside their country, they often turn inward to oppress the people's rebellion using military forces. As a result, human rights have been greatly suppressed.

In Myanmar, for example, amendments were made to its constitution. Revision of the constitution is difficult in Japan, but Myanmar amended its constitution and added a provision banning anyone married to a foreigner, or with children of foreign citizenship, from becoming president. It is unbelievable that such personal matters are included in the constitution, but such amendments were made under the military regime.

A country cannot be necessarily considered a righteous nation with the rule of law just because it has a law system. We cannot say a country is righteous just because there is a parliamentary system either, because if the parliament is full of yes-men, then the country is more or less run by a single power. So, it is not enough just to keep a system running. What matters is the content. It is the matter of the soul.

• On journalism and the Internet society

Democracy is successful only when people have faith in God and Buddha and have a good conscience to be able to judge good and evil because it can allow the good to prevail and the evil to be driven out by the majority of votes.

The same can be said of journalism. If journalists write articles based on their good conscience, even if they may sometimes make mistakes, those with sound opinions, in the long run, will become the majority and gradually change politics and the economy. I believe so. They are bringing down the leaders in power who are possessed by the devil, but that is also their mission.

I think it is right to use paper as a medium and not bullets of guns. But unfortunately, the media are apt to be inclined toward commercialism, so they accuse anyone if it brings them profit. Human rights are sometimes violated along the way.

Also, on the Internet, much less credible information is circulating, and outstanding people or people who are in the limelight of society are shot down by people's jealousy. The Internet does not necessarily bring about a free and democratic society; sometimes, mere private and trifling information causes confusion, leading to chitchat-based politics where politicians only speak ill of others.

Under the teachings of Messiah, develop a value system of good and evil supported by a strong backbone

Overall, we need a value system of good and evil that is supported by a strong backbone. Now is the time when "religious principles," or the "major religious thoughts," must be taught and spread on earth so that people can learn such a value system.

I believe my main mission is to accurately tell apart what is good and what is evil in these ever-changing times and to teach this to people. In this modern age, we cannot judge the current problems with the teachings of God and Buddha that were given 2,000 or 3,000 years ago. So, I can only tell people, with courage, what is right and what is wrong based on what the beings at the level of God and Buddha are now thinking about.

This may lead us to persecution or invite threats from foreign countries. For example, what will happen to countries that try to help Taiwan if China happens to initiate an attack on them to occupy Taiwan? In the case of Japan, videos were posted in China hinting that China would launch nuclear strikes on Japan if Japan intervened to help Taiwan. But Japan should not be a country that will overlook evil acts because of such a threat.

Also, the British aircraft carrier and its strike group made five port calls in Japan in September 2021. The United Kingdom, which is affected by the coronavirus pandemic and sometimes records as many as 50,000 new cases a day despite having many people vaccinated, has dispatched its aircraft carrier and other warships to the other side of the globe.

At the time of the handover of Hong Kong in 1997, the British government returned Hong Kong to China based on the agreement to maintain Hong Kong's liberal system for 50 years. But the promise was broken only after 20-some years. I believe it accords with justice to accuse the Beijing government of breaking an international agreement and to demonstrate military presence to put pressure on China.

Japan, on the other hand, avoids taking a clear stance on the matter and is only concerned about the economic benefit. If the Japanese government, or the Komeito Party and the religious group Soka Gakkai that stick to the government and take pride in contributing to the restoration of Japan-China diplomatic relations, are not yet aware of the changes that are occurring and are avoiding taking political actions, then I must say they are committing acts of evil.

Japan must voice opinions according to its national strength.

It is almost certain that the coronavirus originated in the laboratory in Wuhan. But it is strange that the infection does not spread in the place of origin when other countries are suffering from hundreds of millions of infections. Objectively speaking, this can only be seen as a certain country causing confusion and carrying out massacres against the entire world. If people fail to see this, they must brace themselves for the second and third disasters.

We must be strong.

Before further disasters happen, we need to bring the values of the higher dimension down into this world and spread them. We need to provide people food for thought and teach it. This is important.

We must fight with thoughts and opinions. Before that, we must fight for faith. There is a fight going on between God and the devil. Please know these things.

I do not think it is right for the Japanese people to remain indifferent to world affairs.

This concludes my lecture on the teachings of Messiah.

The Heart of the Earth

Shambhala That Promotes
Spiritual Awakening of Humanity

1

Shambhala: The Secrets of the Earth

In this chapter, I am going to focus on teaching about the spiritual aspect of the mind. I entitled it, "The Heart of the Earth;" in other words, it means the heart of Shambhala. We will be making a movie on this topic in a few years.

Shambhala is a spiritual center of the Earth that is located below Mt. Everest or somewhere around it, and the entrances are in places such as India and Nepal.

When the means of transportation were not as developed as they are today, it was almost impossible to physically go there, but many masters have been there in spiritual form to undergo spiritual training. Some literally go to India or around the Himalayas to undergo yoga training, but those who cannot go there physically have their souls leave their bodies and go there to undergo training during sleep.

If there is a qualification to be a Messiah or savior on Earth, the person has to undergo spiritual training in Shambhala. Of course, there are only a few qualified Messiahs, so many Messiahs-to-be are also there. Those who are at the level of master or guru in each field are given the opportunity to accumulate spiritual training in Shambhala.

This is not necessarily a place you can go to voluntarily; you are called upon or invited to receive training. Those who go there are involved in different specialties or occupations; they need to experience a spiritual awakening in the last stage of attaining mastership in their own field.

The majority of them are naturally religious leaders, but aside from religious leaders, there are also those with different occupations, such as musicians, artists, novelists, inventors, politicians, business people, and, depending on the age, kings, and generals. This place exists to help people attain spiritual awakening, and only a limited number of people can go there.

Once they complete their training there, they often take on the role of guiding people as a master and founder of a group in a limited area or denomination before becoming a savior.

In the olden times, there were such spiritual centers on the continents of Atlantis, Mu, and Lemuria. But after these continents sank into the ocean and vanished from the earth, the spiritual functions have gathered to Shambhala.

To be honest, the neighboring country, China, which mainly focuses on materialistic science, has started a significant battle in this world, so Shambhala has a stronger sense of crisis. If this third dimensional world is filled with people who do not believe in the spiritual world at all, it will be a huge problem. So, there is an urgent need to raise the awareness of the entire Earth. To achieve this, many devote themselves to their training to spread a spiritual culture and a spiritual civilization throughout the world.

Ryunosuke Akutagawa and Yasunari Kawabata[7] are some of the examples of the Japanese authors with whom I now spiritually interact by talking or receiving assistance for our work. These people have access to Shambhala, so they receive a considerable amount of spiritual or mental inspiration. Some of the Japanese Shinto gods also have access to Shambhala.

When people live in this world for long or if they find earth too comfortable to live on, they would feel as if they no longer need the spiritual world, and more and more of them would prefer this world. As a result, they are more concerned about their physical bodies and material lives.

In this modern age, science has advanced, and machine civilization has reached its peak in these 10,000 years. But some factors delude humans in these circumstances.

When humans were living on a more primitive level, people's central concern was how to obtain food. When there were many fights between tribes, people were concerned about how to stop the fight and create peace. Depending on the age, people's concerns differ.

Now that economy has developed, there is a question of how much economic development can contribute to creating a spiritual civilization. If economic development makes people more materialistic and produces more people who are only attached to the earthly way of life, this is a problem.

When we die, we return to the other world. We now live in the third dimension, but there is a realm called the fourth dimension, a part of the Spirit World that has a spiritual field near the surface of the Earth. Today, an increasing number of souls are unable to go beyond this fourth dimension and they repeat reincarnation between the fourth dimension and this world.

This goes for almost all animal spirits, but even among human souls, many have more affection or attachment to life on earth and believe this world is their true home. After leaving this world, they feel they cannot get or do what they want and wish to come back to this world quickly. There is an increasing number of such souls. This is one reason the population of the world has been increasing now.

There are also beings that have come to the Earth all the way from other galaxies. Some of these beings have come to the Earth with the aim of carrying out spiritual and mental training in Shambhala.

There is also the opposite case; some leave Earth for other planets and undergo spiritual training there. This depends on the tendency of the person's soul. Those who have completed their spiritual training on Earth and need to experience different kinds of training will go to other training planets and accumulate training there under a great master.

In this sense, Shambhala is the spiritual center of the Earth. Some beings come to the Earth from outer space to accumulate spiritual training in Shambhala. But a large part of Shambhala is veiled in mystery and its secrets almost never go out.

In recent times, starting around the 1800s, some of the secrets of Shambhala came out in the form of Theosophy. But because it was the time when the world was modernizing and the material, scientific civilization was developing, those who taught the secrets of Shambhala were persecuted and dismissed in this world as being fraud or deceiving.

Even so, the secrets of Shambhala have always affected various religions of the world under the surface. Living in this world is like a floating weed, but the secrets of Shambhala played an important role for the floating weed-like religions to grow their root and take root in the soil at the bottom of the water.

2

Initiation to Become a Messiah

A Messiah fully understands the spiritual truths

Initiation (for spiritual awakening) is necessary for those aiming to be a Messiah. One cannot be a true Messiah without undergoing initiation. Even the many masters who are at the stage before Messiahs need to undergo initiation.

What is this initiation?

It is extensive training to fully understand that the spiritual world is the true home of our souls and that soul training—in other words, the training of the mind, which is the core part of the soul—is the very reason why humans are living on this Earth as advanced animals.

To put this in worldly terms, it can be something like the ascetic training Shakyamuni Buddha underwent in India before attaining enlightenment. Some people stop eating grains and go on a fast, whereas some undergo difficult training others don't think they can possibly do. Even now, some people take on ascetic practice in Japan by walking in the mountains or sitting under the waterfall. They do not intend to become an Olympic athlete, so it is not the ascetic practice itself that is important. Through such training, they are trying to strengthen their spiritual senses over physical senses. That is the main purpose of their training.

Fasting entails danger, but it is possible to practice fasting using established methods under good guidance. When you are fasting, you will surely experience a moment when your spiritual body is detached from your physical body. At such times, you will become aware that you are a spiritual being.

But then, you will also experience a kind of evil temptation. As you detach from your physical body and begin to understand that you are a spiritual being, you will definitely be approached by an evil temptation that will try to delude you in many ways.

Those that delude you are the beings of the Spirit World. They are beings who still believe that this world is their true home even after they have become spirits, and they want to make others think the same as them. These beings of evil nature will appear and try to lure you with worldly temptations.

The desires for food, sex, and sleep are the typical, basic desires that humans naturally have as they lead a physical life. Various beings of evil nature will come to you through these desires.

Animal spirits can hardly escape the world of those desires, but some of them have spiritual powers and are revered as gods in many places. For example, some shrines and temples worship beings who grant worldly benefits.

People pray for many things, including abundant harvest, successful marriage, or being blessed with children. In Japan, Inari (fox spirits) shrines are famous for such worship.

If people have lust-related wishes, they may sometimes receive power from snake spirits, in addition to fox spirits, because snake spirits have a strong sense of attachment. When they fail to realize people's wishes, the spirits' power can turn into a spell that curses the target person to death. In this way, some spirits try to unite men and women using people's fear. Animal spirits like these sometimes transform themselves and appear as beings of evil nature.

There are also cases where human spirits have turned into something different. They had a very strong desire when they were living as humans, and after death, they remain in the fourth dimension in the form that manifests their desire. There are many such beings. They repeat reincarnation between this place and the world on earth, and this cycle is generally called the "reincarnation between the Realms of Desire."

Among those who repeat such reincarnations, strong beings have appeared and become the kings and devils of hell. There are also others who reside in the rear part of heaven and have acquired special abilities. They claim themselves to be gods and use their power to, as they say, make people "worship" them or, from other people's perspectives, delude people.

As you train yourself in this world to become spiritual, you will definitely be faced with evil temptations, which will put you in a difficult situation. As a result, you will be tested along the way to see how deeply you are convinced that you are a spiritual being.

The spiritual training
to attain the enlightenment of the universe

If you undergo spiritual training for a long time in Shambhala, you can experience a spiritual awakening at a relatively early stage. There can be many different ways of training, and as you undergo training, you can sometimes hear or see spirits or acquire special abilities. But these abilities alone do not necessarily lead to your enlightenment. These abilities can manifest as one of the ways to prove your enlightenment, but these spiritual phenomena themselves are not enlightenment.

What matters is how deeply you are aware that you are spiritual energy. While you live in a physical body in this world, you need to seek the mental attitude, the spiritual training, and the heart of enlightenment that you had been seeking in heaven. In the process of making efforts to attain such a state of mind in this world, your soul is being polished.

In other words, having a physical body and having to eat to survive in this world is like an obstacle race. There are things that you can easily overcome by becoming spiritual. But in this world, they would be obstacles.

For example, a human cannot cross the threshold of other people's house or room without notice or permission, but as a spirit, it does not matter whether it is a house or not; you can pass through a house or a room even without opening the door. We are living in such a mysterious world.

Some may say that everything should be revealed for the living people to be spiritual, but in that case, there would be no need for people to be born into this world. They can just stay in the Spirit World.

In the Spirit World, there are no traffic accidents as we have in this world. At a glance, spirits may appear as if they are about to bump into each other. But what we'll see is them just passing through each other. There are buildings and other things in the Spirit World, but we can pass through anything.

We can pass through mountains as well. Even if we think we may hit a mountain as we fly in the sky, we actually won't; the mountain will split before us, and a path will open up for us to pass through. Even if we fall into a lake and think we may drown to death, we won't; we won't drown even if we don't breathe air. We will have such mysterious experiences. I presume many mysterious stories of ancient times include these kinds of spiritual experiences.

For the same reason, those who can go beyond the Spirit World of Earth in a spiritual form can travel through space even if there is no oxygen. They can arrive at a planet where there is no oxygen or food and interact with the beings of the Spirit World there.

It is said that the speed of light is the highest speed and the distance between planets is calculated by the speed of light. A planet is then described as being some light-years away or hundreds of light-years away, for example. A light-year means the distance light travels in one Earth year. It is said that apart from the planets in our solar system, a planet inhabited by humanoids in another star system is at least four light-years away. So, it takes at least four years to get there when traveling at the speed of light.

However, there is no limit to spiritual speed. The spiritual speed varies according to the person's spiritual power and the power of his or her enlightenment. Some can travel at the speed of light, whereas others can travel at the speed of sound. Those with a lower awareness can only travel at the speed of an earthly human walking or running.

The will-o'-the-wisp, or ignis fatuus, that you may sometimes see is usually flying waveringly at the speed of a child walking. So, flying at the speed of a bicycle is actually very fast for the will-o'-the-wisp.

The more you are awakened to your spirituality and the more you understand that your soul is free and shapeless, the more you can change your form and the faster you can travel. In some cases, you can get to a distant place almost in an instant.

Masters and those referred to as "adepts"—the awakened gurus at a slightly higher level than masters—can get to a planet that is four light-years away and inhabited by other humanoid space beings almost in an instant. As soon as they think of their destination, they can instantly arrive there.

Then, how about traveling to another galaxy further away? It is not easy for an individual spirit divided from one soul group to go to a distant galaxy independently. So, the spirit can amass all the members of its soul group to form a ball of light to move from one galaxy to another.

The speed at which a ball of light can travel differs from others. Some will spend years to get to their destination while others only a couple of days. Some travel in a matter of a few hours, yet others appear to arrive in an instant by traveling at ultrahigh speed. This depends on the ability of each soul group. To travel to a distant place, which often entails a lot of difficulties, you usually need to gather all the members of your soul group that are now independent spirits. This is the basic style.

Other than these, when an individual spirit experiences traveling to outer space or going to other planets, a higher guiding spirit will normally accompany it and guide it. Otherwise, the spirit will be lost in space and become a wanderer. To prevent the spirit from losing itself in the vast universe, a high spirit will come to guide it.

There is such enlightenment of the universe in which you attain complete freedom. In Shambhala on Earth, many are undergoing spiritual training to become such enlightened ones.

El Cantare, the Master of Shambhala that produces qualified saviors

Coming back to the issues of this world, China has become a nation of materialistic science and is threatening India and its surrounding countries. They try to invade parts of India and other areas surrounding Mt. Everest, but there is a strong power at work to protect these areas. From now on, many incidents will occur that will make it clear to the eyes of people, "Which is the true world—the Spirit World or the world on earth?"

The Master or the top leader of Shambhala on Earth is El Cantare—the part of El Cantare that does not appear in this world. It is this part of Him who is the Master of

Shambhala. There still are a lot of secrets regarding this, and not everything can be revealed now. When Shakyamuni Buddha was born near the border between Nepal and India and spread Buddhism in Nepal and India, Shambhala was almost determined to be the spiritual center of the Earth.

Before that, other places were the centers. Egypt, for example, used to be the main spiritual center for a long time, and it served as a training ground. But when the Ptolemaic Dynasty was destroyed about 2,000 years ago, its spiritual center weakened substantially. There still is a field, but it has become weak. The civilization of Egypt has become a thing of the past.

There was once a time when Israel was the center, but now it has lost its power, too. Before that, many civilizations arose around the Tigris and Euphrates and many qualified saviors were born. But, as you can see, these areas are no longer advanced countries. They are surrounded by the desert, and they lost their major position as a spiritual center. There still is a ground for ethnic gods to undergo spiritual training, but it has been losing a lot of power as the global-level training ground.

There was also a time when Europe was at its height. Nearly 10,000 years ago, God Odin was revered mainly in Northern Europe. Since then, until the Celtic civilization was virtually ruined, Northern Europe had been the spiritual center. Greece was also once a spiritual center in Europe in such a way. The spiritual field shifts with the rise and fall of civilizations.

Currently, in a worldly context, Shambhala is located beneath Mt. Everest, but because the spiritual center shifts in tandem with the rise and fall of civilizations on earth, Happy Science voices its opinions on the development of international politics and economics and wars on earth.

There was once an advanced civilization and a spiritual center in Atlantis, but when the Atlantis civilization was destroyed, the gods in those times had no choice but to choose other places to be born into. The same was true when the Mu continent sank into the ocean, as was the case with the Lemuria civilization that flourished around the Indian Ocean—between India and Africa—but eventually sank.

There was a time when what is now called Africa flourished and was the spiritual center, but unfortunately, since the center of civilization moved to other places, it is no longer so spiritually attractive.

Shambhala and the awakened ones
1) Jesus Christ during his youth

As described in some of Happy Science books, Jesus Christ set out on a journey of spiritual training and went to Shambhala when he was still alive (see *The Golden Laws*).

Jesus Christ appeared before people when he was around the age of 30 and preached his teachings for about three years until he was crucified around the age of 33. In the 33 years of his life, there are 17 mysterious years. It is not known what he had been doing before he became 30.

It is clear that he had been to Egypt for a time. In Egypt, he learned from the temple priests and also studied the ancient literature that had been handed down from the time of the Atlantis civilization at a large library. Buddhism had already reached Egypt in those times, and there were Buddhist temples as well. Jesus knew that there was a higher spiritual field and a higher religion in India, so he traveled to Western India and learned a part of Buddhism and yoga of those times.

Shambhala and the awakened ones
2) John Lennon and Lao-tzu

More recently, John Lennon did something similar. Happy Science pointed out for the first time that John Lennon—the leader of The Beatles—is part of the soul of Jesus Christ. He now often appears at Happy Science to help with our music.

John Lennon was born in Liverpool and carried out his musical activities all around England and other places, such as Germany, but his life changed along the way. At some point in life, he had to undergo spiritual training to become an adept. So, he took trains to travel toward India. Around that time, he left his first wife. He then started yoga training and had some shocking spiritual experiences in India.

By the time he married a Japanese woman, Yoko Ono, he was no longer the John Lennon he used to be. He became a different person after receiving an oriental initiation. So, he grew apart from the other members of The Beatles. I suppose he was drawn to his original mission.

In this world, he could not completely fulfill that mission; he was only able to show the introductory part of it. But spiritually, he resumed his work again recently.

As did Jesus, John Lennon also went to India to attain spiritual awakening. This is worth noting.

In China, it is said that Lao-tzu had gone across Hangu Pass in Western China and disappeared into the desert, never to be seen again. Actually, he went to Shambhala after that. It seems his soul still mainly lives in that area.

Shambhala and the awakened ones
3) Newton and Einstein

There are many other awakened ones who attained spiritual awakening in the past civilizations, but you may not know them. Because their names and activities are not handed down, it is almost impossible to know about them directly. But there are such beings.

To take another example, Newton established Newtonian mechanics and is regarded as the father of modern science. In this world, he was quite successful; he worked for the government and served as the Master of the Royal Mint. But behind the scenes, he was a kind of occultist and devoted himself to exploring mystical phenomena. It is said that there is an underground organization called Freemasonry, and Newton is said to have been its true founder behind the scenes or its first Grand Master.

Outwardly, he was a prominent physicist that created Newtonian mechanics. He wondered why an apple fell from a tree and discovered gravity. From there, he laid the foundation for classical mechanics and physics. In other words, he unveiled part of the secrets of God.

After that, about 100 years ago, Einstein appeared and established new modern physics that surpassed Newtonian mechanics. Even the physics that Einstein formulated 100 years ago contains elements that are still too difficult for modern people to comprehend.

Thus, gurus or adepts who work in the fields of science and mathematics are also in Shambhala. One of Newton's names that people do not know is Koot Hoomi. Koot Hoomi is in Shambhala; he controls the development of science and technology on Earth and is giving spiritual revelation to people.

There are many other gurus that are not known to you, but they will make their appearance as the need arises. If you seek for spiritual awakening more earnestly by being freed from physical bondage, these beings will probably appear as guiding spirits. But the key to opening the door to such a world will not be given to you unless you become capable of controlling your desire for worldly benefits or the Six Worldly Delusions. It will not be given as long as many of you feel you are deprived of freedom and find it absurd and unfair if you are given precept-like rules to control your actions or your desire for self-realization. If you stumble at such a primitive level, unfortunately, it will be very difficult to enter the world of mastery.

Shambhala and the awakened ones
4) Hermes and Ophealis who give power to Shambhala

Among the soul siblings of El Cantare, Hermes was active in the fields of politics, economics, and the military, and he worked to promote trade and economy in this world. But he is also said to be playing the role of guidance and communication to bridge this world and the other world. A part of Hermes' role now is to give power to Shambhala.

A little earlier than this current age, during the age of the 12 Olympian gods, there used to be a large spiritual field centering around Olympus, and Hermes was active there around that time. But after Shakyamuni Buddha was born on earth, Hermes has been visiting Shambhala more often.

Before Hermes, another soul sibling of El Cantare was born under the name Ophealis, otherwise known as Osiris. It is said that Ophealis became the king of the underworld after death. For a long time, he had worked to grant spiritual secrets in Egypt but has now moved to Shambhala after the fall of Egypt.

Shambhala and the awakened ones
5) The strong belief Jesus gained
after his spiritual awakening in Shambhala

There are many other topics to discuss. In Christianity, for example, if you put aside the work of the Christian churches that spread in this world and only pick up the words of Jesus in the Bible, you will probably notice that there are many spiritual elements that are not of this world. Jesus spoke the words that would overturn worldly values completely, which is typical of those who have received initiation and attained spiritual awakening in Shambhala. That is why his words cannot be completely understood from the perspective of this world only.

Viewed from the worldly perspective, there was a very twisted side to his words and deeds that many Christians probably cannot understand. For example, Jesus said, "If you say to this mountain, 'Be taken up and thrown into the sea,' ...it will be done for you." This is hard to understand in this world.

However, those referred to as "adepts" truly have the power to crumble the mountain in the Spirit World. They can even change their form. In the Spirit World, too, there are many different things, including landscape, buildings, and the spirits living in them. The adepts truly have the power to change these things completely.

Jesus chose to be crucified, knowing he would lose his life on earth, and some people may see it as being weak in worldly intelligence and say that Jesus did not have a strong will to live or lacked the wisdom to survive. But this is a matter of spiritual awakening.

For those who believe 100 percent in the existence of the soul and the mind, which is the core part of the soul, and who have 100 percent confidence in controlling their minds, living spiritually is all that matters and everything in this world is just an extra. This is beyond the comprehension of the disciples, but masters are different in this context.

Shambhala and the awakened ones
6) Socrates and Plato who had experiences in the Spirit World

Apart from Jesus, there were others who acted in a way that appears to be treating their lives lightly, and their deeds were sometimes regarded as foolish or stupid at a glance. But some of them actually grasped their spiritual self as their true entity in their everyday lives.

Socrates, too, was such a man. He, himself, had a spiritual ability and he taught about reincarnation into the Spirit World. His philosophy became the basis of Greek philosophy. And if his thoughts have been handed down to this day, the idea of reincarnation must still live in Western society. But the scholars and philosophers of later generations cannot understand those teachings of Socrates at all and are skeptical of such an idea.

Socrates talked about being reborn in the other world. He also taught that reincarnation between the spirit worlds of animals and humans is possible. For example, those who had the virtue of courage in this world can be reborn in the form of a lion, or those who were strongly aware of their innocence in this world and want to show it can be reborn as a swan. Such descriptions still remain, but they are taken as mere metaphors, allegories, or old tales. This is very unfortunate.

People dismissed these descriptions as old stories, and currently, from the 20th century onward, philosophy has largely become the mere study of symbolic logic or has been combined with mathematics. Unfortunately, this is far from attaining the secrets of life. Both Socrates and his disciple Plato had the spiritual ability and had many experiences of the Spirit World.

3

Gaining Back the Heart of Shambhala

Undermining materialistic tendency in modern society

Today is a very difficult time; we are significantly affected by materialistic civilization and worldly education. Even though someone like Jung was sent from heaven to reveal some of the secrets of the Spirit World, Jungian psychology has become connected to materialistic medicine and has obscured the truth about the existence of the Spirit World. Jungian psychologists tend to explain dreams and the Spirit World as mere symbols, and they do not necessarily believe in the existence of the Spirit World.

Even so, psychologists are regarded as superior to religious leaders who believe in the Spirit World and are mistakenly believed to know well about the human brain and mind. Such a misunderstanding prevails and people below are overtaking the upper people. So, we need to correct the current structure of academics.

Taking an example from modern philosophy, Descartes also had a spiritual ability, as you can see from his work. He was a very spiritual person and received inspiration. He could often see spirits and had out-of-body experiences.

However, some people started to take his philosophy just superficially and too literally and understood his work such as *Discourse on the Method* as a very rational and logical idea.

In a similar vein, Kant appeared in Germany. Although he, himself, was interested in the Spirit World, he could not have many spiritual experiences; as he lived through the age of the Industrial Revolution, he became more immersed in modern reason. As a result, people came to value reason, which led them to seek rational ways of thinking or logical ways of thinking by training their brains.

But this has nothing to do with enlightenment. Enlightenment is above all this. Material things and technologies of this world, and the various explanations based on them—such as an idea that "global warming melts glaciers," "Earth's temperature is rising," or "global warming is due to the increase in CO_2 emissions"—are physical matters below enlightenment; they are not metaphysical matters. Such physical ways of thinking are actually based on Kant's rationalism. Because people neglect spiritual factors or aspects of the other world, they believe that only what can be explained in this world is correct.

This is why, in this modern age, you cannot get a doctorate, for instance, unless you are rational and logical. There is a tendency not to acknowledge anything spiritual or inspirational.

Inspiration was the core value in Edison's life. As an inventor, he was a genius, and he lived independently of the academic world, which was good. If someone like him had attended a graduate school of the prestigious university of today and studied to earn a doctorate, that person would have definitely been crushed.

It is wrong to say that only those ideas that can be explained in a worldly way for everyone to understand are valuable. The current civilization is mainly based on the six-dimensional principles that can be understood and explained by scholar-like intelligence; the principles of the seventh dimension and above are not adopted enough. This is the problem. So, I believe it is very important to undermine the basis of this civilization by telling people spiritual values, such as theosophical or other ideas that can sometimes be ridiculed as occultism.

Kant, whom I mentioned earlier, did have faith in God, but he contributed to weakening God's power to govern this world because he placed greater value on human thoughts. He omitted matters that cannot be dealt with academically and instead focused on explaining and thinking about matters that can be discussed on the academic level. But it was not that he dismissed anything spiritual.

Among his contemporaries, there was Swedenborg, who had supernatural and spiritual abilities. Swedenborg spiritually saw a fire burning at a distant place at the same time as it occurred, traveled to the Spirit World for days while leaving his physical body in suspended animation, and described his journey in the Spirit World. He also glimpsed a kind of scroll or note that described each person's destiny and wrote these experiences. Kant took interest in the works of Swedenborg and would actually read them. But he thought he should not step into matters that he could not experience for himself or experiment on. His attitude of holding back worked to put limitations on modern academics.

In this regard, Ryuho Okawa is now putting out various ideas to create a brand-new academic structure, thereby trying to expand the current academic structure that fails to surpass the realm of the sixth dimension to the realm of the ninth dimension and beyond.

Protect Shambhala from China through two kinds of revolutions

What I want you to know now is that there is a place for spiritual awakening called Shambhala. Should there be a new rise and fall of civilizations on earth and should the current Shambhala no longer remain suitable for spiritual training, another spiritual center must be created on Earth. No one probably has ever thought of such a thing, but this is a very important issue.

In ancient China, Tao Yuanming[8] described the Peach Blossom Land (utopia). This Peach Blossom Land is also an entrance to Shambhala. China in those times was still very rich in spirituality. Confucianism, Taoism, Buddhism, and other philosophies still had a strong influence, and China had great significance in terms of spirituality. But now that China is becoming a huge country with no spiritual significance, it seems the path to Shambhala is about to be closed.

The Peach Blossom Land is said to have been at the recess of a mountain that people who had fled from the tyranny of the first emperor of the Qin Dynasty found. People settled there and created a utopia for centuries. It started during the time of the first Qin emperor and still existed during the age of the Three Kingdoms. You may have heard of the name Doutei-ko nyan-nyan or the goddess Lake Dongting. The entrance to the Peach Blossom Land was actually not very far from Lake Dongting. But we can't find it anymore.

A lot of activities to destroy spiritual fields have been carried out, and various natural disasters have taken place against them. So, the battle has been going on. It would be quite unbearable if the vast land of China completely ceases to function as a spiritual field. So, we have to prevent this at any cost.

Confucius, who started Confucianism, did not teach much about spiritual matters, and that is why Confucianism is misused now in the same way that the philosophy of Kant has been used to deny the existence of the Spirit World.

Confucianism had the philosophy of Tian (heaven) and the idea of Tiandi (emperor in heaven). It taught the moral or the ruling of the world by a virtuous person based on Tiandi's teachings. But the spiritual aspect has been omitted from Confucianism, and it has been misused for a long time by the politicians just to control the people and to maintain order and stability in this world. Confucius is now facing a difficult situation, so Confucianism is on the verge of destruction. This teaches that religion must not be too realistic or materialistic.

Thus, you are now carrying out both this-worldly revolution and the spiritual revolution. In doing so, you need this philosophy of Shambhala.

There is more to be disclosed about the world of secrets

I said that Newton was the first Grand Master of Freemasonry, but the roots of Freemasonry can be traced back to even before the time of Newton. During the Renaissance period,

Rosicrucianism and the like were popular around Italy, which later gave birth to Freemasonry. Around those times, Hermeticism was widespread.

There was a lot of research on the teachings of Hermes Trismegistus, who was said to have been born in ancient Egypt more than 3,000 years ago. His teachings led to the development of alchemy and others, laying the groundwork for modern chemistry.

Hermeticism was passed down to Newton; then Newton's Freemasonry became associated with various leaders of the world, including those who would serve as president or prime minister. In Japan, it is said that Ryoma Sakamoto[9], who was mainly active in the Glover Residence in Nagasaki prefecture, was one of the members of Japan's Freemasonry, and he is said to have received financial support from Freemasonry.

Freemasonry still exists today, though it has lost momentum. I think religions themselves such as Christianity have more power now. But when churches are involved in worldly affairs too much and become politics-oriented, secret groups such as Freemasonry may gain the power to connect people underground.

There is much more to be disclosed about the world of secrets. Please know that not all secrets have been revealed. I have talked about the Heart of the Earth to compile *The Laws Of Messiah*. This is also the Heart of Shambhala.

I hope you will advance in your enlightenment, so I can reveal higher teachings.

The Love of Messiah

Love on Earth,
the Training Ground for the Souls

1

Why Messiah Exists—
Thinking from the Way This World Works

Even great souls start from scratch in this world

The theme of this chapter is a very unusual and difficult one. It is on "The Love of Messiah." How much of it can I teach—I'll try to teach as much as possible even with the limitation of human words.

Now, as for why a Messiah exists, the answer has to do with the way this world works.

Before humans are born into this world, they live as a spirit, as a soul, in the Real World, also known as another world. Some are reborn into this world as quickly as in a couple of years or a few decades after death, but the usual reincarnation cycle is once in several hundred years. In the case of those with an important mission, they are born only once in 1,000 years, 2,000 years, or 3,000 years.

The fact is that the spiritual world beyond this world is the Real World. And there is a rule to our reincarnation. When we are born into this world, everyone receives a physical body from their parents. They might weigh 3,000 grams or 4,000 grams as a baby, but all of us reside as a soul in this tiny body. And the rule on Earth is that "You forget your past lives for the time being."

If there was no such rule, there would be people who are born and say, "In my previous life, I was so-and-so born in a neighboring village. My father and mother at the time were like this, these were their names, and I died at this young age from this illness, so I am reborn." Although rare, there are reports of these kinds of cases in India and other such places.

This sounds like a blessing, but if you were reborn into this world and your parents in your previous life were still alive, you would feel unsure about who your parents are. You would go back and forth between them, and your identity would not be very clear. This can happen. So, to maximize the gains from studying in this world, the rule is set: "Each person's life is reset to zero when they are born."

That is why everyone is born into this world as a baby, with no clue as to what will become of them. But as people live for a few decades, they will come to know who they truly are and understand what they must do in this world. This is the kind of experience we are expected to accumulate.

In that sense, it is also expected that you make mistakes to a certain extent.

You may imagine that if someone who had achieved great success in their past life were born with that wisdom, he would make very few mistakes in this lifetime. But everyone is made to forget everything when they are born. We must start from zero, struggling to utter a word until we are one year old and enduring a time when we can't even say, "Dadda, Mamma." Some babies are quick to start crawling; others are not. Some babies take longer than others to stand and walk on their own. Some children are not good at learning or do not behave well before they come of school age. Children grow up differently under a variety of conditions.

One characteristic about today's times is that you never know what kind of soul will be born where. The class system has collapsed and receded all over the world, making it possible even for great souls to be born in various places and start from scratch as an "experiment." Today's modern era is different from the past in that it is possible to take up any kind of occupation or, depending on how you study, to go to any kind of school, work at any kind of company, and do all kinds of things.

With that being said, the class system does have its practical uses. For example, a soul that wants to take up a certain occupation can inherit it by choosing to be born to parents who are in that occupation. A typical example is to be born into a family of politicians and become a second-generation or third-generation politician. There aren't many families like that, but it can give a soul a better chance of becoming a politician. There can also be a culture in the family or at home that makes it easier to take on a particular occupation, though some people can't fulfill their ambitions even with these advantages.

In Japan too, up until about the Edo period, if you were born as a child of a doctor, it was still possible to automatically take over the family practice. But today, a child born to farmers, a child born to shopkeepers, or a child born to an office worker can also become a doctor if they study, by entering medical school and passing the national medical licensing exam.

On the other hand, there are people whose father or mother puts people through a lot of grief because of a crime they committed or a mistake they made. These people may wish to turn over a new leaf and aspire for a completely different profession, such as a police officer who adheres to the law, a judge, a prosecutor or lawyer, or a doctor or nurse who can help others. There are also such cases.

Problems in the family, therefore, will not necessarily lead to a person's downfall. Some people will aspire for the opposite. That option is also provided.

Examples of how poverty can change across ages and regions

The world today has become such a convenient place that it is a very enviable time for people born in other eras. That's why many souls wish to be born in the present age. Many souls are curious to know, "What is the world like now?" and want to gain new experiences.

But this-worldly convenience has also become a condition that makes it easy for people to forget that the other world is the Real World and their original home. That is the difficult part.

• Beggars and barefoot children in India

During the times when there were long periods of poverty, just living from day to day was such a struggle that some people resorted to begging to have food to eat.

I think India today has become a little more affluent than the time when I first traveled there. But when I first visited Sarnath—the place where Shakyamuni Buddha gave his first sermon to his five initial disciples after attaining enlightenment—I saw children who were missing an arm or a leg. They came limping or crawling toward me saying, "Please give me money."

"Were they born like this?" I asked the guide and the guide told me, "It's not always the case. Parents cut off an arm or a leg out of love for their children to give them a way to eat. If children beg for money with an obvious disability like that, people will feel sympathy and think, 'How could they possibly work?' And they give them money. So, sometimes parents do such a thing." I was surprised to know that such a form of love existed. There are places where parents make their children disabled so they can live on the charity of others.

I suppose things are a little different now, but the first time I went to India, which was more than a couple dozen years ago, the children of farmers did not have any footwear. They were barefoot as they worked in the fields or rice paddies. Nearby was a road being paved with asphalt. Upon this freshly laid, still hot and sticky pavement, a girl was walking barefoot, making me feel, "It's such a pity they don't even have sandals to wear."

Farmers usually have children because they can have their children help with their work. From when the children are still young, such as elementary or middle school age, they can begin to help with the farm work. The more children, the more help they get. I have heard that this is why half the children in India can't go to school. I do not know if it is still the same today; I want to believe that things have become a little better now.

There were eras when people struggled even to be born into this world or to raise a family. But as society develops, people start to enjoy plentiful food. In advanced countries, about 10-20 percent of food is probably thrown away without being eaten.

I think about 800 million to a billion people now suffer from hunger in the world, but it is said that if all the uneaten food were collected around the world, then these people would have enough to eat. On one hand, food is thrown away; on the other hand, people are dying from starvation.

In poor regions, a primitive form of economics also prevails: stealing, robbing, and killing as a way to get things or, as done from a long time ago, women selling their bodies. Of course, the same practices can be seen in advanced countries as well.

• Homeless people reading newspapers in Japan

Japan today is experiencing many natural disasters. It is also an age when a plague has broken out in the form of the novel coronavirus infection. Even so, as far as we can see, there are scarcely any beggars in Japan.

I have seen in the past—not recently—two or three homeless people living outside using cardboard boxes in front of the entrance of Shinjuku Gyoen (a national garden in Tokyo). It was hard to tell whether they were living that way because they were truly poor or they were just enjoying the hippie lifestyle. Even back then, there were stories of such homeless people having diabetes or reading a newspaper while living under the girder. These stories surprised the people of other developed countries.

The literacy rate is high in Japan. Everyone can read as education is compulsory until junior high school. But in many other countries, there are still many people who cannot read. People need proper education to be able to read a newspaper.

Moreover, the homeless people in Japan can get leftovers. They can get food that has passed its "sell-by" time from convenience stores or restaurants. Having the academic ability to read newspapers means having the ability to work somewhere. There are people like that among the homeless people.

Even though a certain number of people are unemployed, they receive welfare from the government, and various kinds of help and support. They may have some savings, so they do not go as far as to beg for money or food. This may be a form of an evolved society.

This world is a place for soul training, and life is a workbook

Communism has been widely criticized. I often criticize it too, but in the last 100 years, communism has spread to a certain number of people despite it. So, those on the opposing side, or the liberal camp, also have to adopt communist policies or else risk losing votes.

By "communist policy," I mean social welfare. It is not possible to make everyone equal by communalizing everyone's personal property, so as an alternative to communism, advanced countries are trying to even out the income disparity that arises from individuals working hard and becoming wealthy. They are taking away money from high-earners and those with a lot of wealth by way of taxes and other means and giving it to those who have difficulty making a living. This means that advanced countries are adopting communism-like policies.

Whether information is accurate or not differs depending on the situation of each country. Also, in some military dictatorships, poverty and illness are widespread because control has become the objective and people are unable to prosper through free, economic activities.

What I have to say here is, as I said earlier, "This world is essentially a place for soul training. For the poor or the rich, the powerless or the powerful, this world has been equally provided as a place for training one's soul. You have been given a 'workbook of problems' to be solved and you are being asked, 'How will you choose to live under these circumstances?'"

Those born in peacetime might be blessed with happiness. Those born in wartime might have no choice but to desperately fight for their lives or escape as best as they can while bullets fly and gunshots go off.

Wars from now on not only could involve killing specific people but also could be fought by erasing whole cities in an instant with large, nuclear weapons or other bombs and missiles. For some, their life could be over by the time they realize it. As time changes, the way of life on earth can vary.

2

What Human Beings Must Not Lose Sight of through Soul Experiences

People who are very self-centered and possessive can become "worse than an animal"

Through different civilizations and cultures, war and peacetime, and in-between periods, the soul gains all kinds of experiences. What I wish for you to learn through them all is, "No matter what circumstance you are in, explore how you must live as a human being with a soul." In other words, "Do not lose sight of your spirituality" or "Do not lose sight of yourself as a spiritual entity."

Spirituality can be easily lost even amid prosperity. Having too much money, being rich, or holding great power can cause you to lose sight of it. Likewise, poverty can cause you to fall into a kind of materialism where material things become everything to you.

When you're living at the minimum level, securing food to eat becomes all that matters. Your way of life becomes animalistic, and day after day, you think about food only. Animals think about eating and about how to get away or protect themselves to not be eaten. The worst for them is to be eaten or to be killed, so they are satisfied with just being able to eat. This is the everyday experience in the animal world.

Under these circumstances, they make all kinds of efforts. Some have developed what could be considered weapons; they have grown fangs or horns. Hedgehogs grow needles. Others can dive into the water, fly in the air, or run fast on the ground. Each has been given some kind of feature that allows them to protect themselves or to survive.

Preservation of life in this world is the minimum basic goal for human beings as well, but how far you can go beyond just surviving like an animal is also important. I said, "surviving like an animal." In this regard, I often teach, "Don't be self-centered. Don't be selfish." This is because being selfish is something animals and humans can do naturally. When you are born into this world and grow up in it, you cannot help but become selfish. You want to secure food. Your life is dear to you. You would rather that someone else die than for it to be you. If there is food for only one person when there are two, you want to be the one to have it. You want a house, you want a job, and you want many other things. All this is very normal, and you are bound to become this way because of your instincts. You become this way also by an extension of your animalistic aspects.

But there are times when human beings become worse than animals.

Animals, even predators, will stop eating once their stomach is full. Lions, when on the hunt, will chase antelopes or zebras in groups and attack and eat them, but once they eat and are full, they stop hunting. Sometimes prey animals run by a lion stretched out on the ground and nothing happens. Even prey animals know this. A lion can probably go without eating for four days after it has eaten.

Human beings, however, don't stop at a full stomach. Their desires tend to grow. They want to store food for the future or want more of what generates food, such as money and other sources of wealth. If there is a limited amount of it, they want to monopolize it or control it in an oligopoly and keep it in the family.

Some store owners think, "I want more customers to come to my store even if it means other places will go out of business." When people start a business, their business goal is usually growth, but some wish for their company to grow bigger even at the expense of other companies. When a big company emerges, many other companies are actually out of business. In some cases, companies deliberately trigger a product shortage and hike up prices to make a huge profit for themselves.

The problem of today's higher education, as seen in people's choice in occupation

One of the popular jobs today in Japan is to work for a foreign-affiliated company. Among the people who went abroad to study the how-tos of management and finance, many seem to be engaging less in the regular work of producing and selling an actual product or earning by rendering a service. Instead, they buy a weak company for a trifle, hike up the company's stock price by cutting personnel, and then, once the company value goes up, sell it a year later. This is a part of what is often called M&A (mergers and acquisitions); profit is made by buying companies, raising their stock prices, and then selling them off. Some people make this their job, and many of those who are considered smart seem to be heading in this direction.

As a result, the ranking of college popularity is said to have changed. In the past, graduating from the Faculty of Law of the University of Tokyo and becoming a government official was considered to be the fast track to success, and this was a popular path. But now, it is said that you can get a higher income by going to a faculty of economics and working for an international company, and this path is gaining popularity. There are also people who try to make money not through proper business but by playing with fictitious numbers and profiting from their rise and fall, as I mentioned earlier. A lot of smart people are going down that path.

It must feel more advanced to use mathematics to make money than to barter as primitive people used to, but I feel there is something that is not quite heavenly in that kind of work.

People used to create a company and work for decades with the aim of making the world more affluent or convenient through their products or of making everyone's life better or easier through the service they provide. But as I hear that this is no longer what people aspire for, that their aim is now just to keep their profits, and that smart people are heading toward such a line of work, I am a little concerned about the future.

What's more, some people choose to go to medical school just because they are smart. The faculty of medicine in each Japanese university has an enrollment limit of about 100 students, so the total number of accepted students nationwide will not exceed 10,000. It's fine to limit the number of enrollments that way to protect the profession. But among those people who choose to go to medical school simply because they are smart, a large number of them are not fit to be a doctor.

Some people aim to be doctors because they think, "I want to save lives" or "I want to heal the sick." They may have had someone in their family who died of an illness, died in an accident, or suffered a great injury but was saved by medical treatment. Or, they may have had an experience of being hospitalized or treated at a hospital. These people have the wish to help others, which is a merciful heart of a bodhisattva or an angel. However, if people want to go to medical school just because it's a prestigious school or because they just want to prove how smart they are, then they would not be very different from the people who make money off of buying and selling companies.

If you choose your occupation just because it pays well or proves your academic level, then your choice may have nothing to do with the true purpose of the occupation.

I often think about what it means to be truly smart. If people believe that being smart means becoming like an AI, then human beings could really end up becoming like machines. Work done by human hands can have a lot of mistakes. These mistakes can be decreased when the work is carried out by precise machines. But this could lead people to think that machines are greater than human beings because they don't make mistakes.

Although greater precision is certainly helpful in doing practical work, I feel this view would lead human beings to lose sight of their mind. When human beings become closer to AI, or something like an add-on to a computer, I think many people will forget what the mind is.

As I talk to people with strong academic backgrounds, I find some of them have so much specialized knowledge and know-how that it makes me feel as if they really are like machines. It makes me wonder, "Where has their mind gone?" The education system in Japan today has already lost sight of the mind and often does not teach it. Even in countries that have faith and have a national religion, more time is spent on teaching about worldly knowledge and technical matters than on teaching about the mind in their higher education.

There is a famous movie that touches on this theme. It's a story from the United States. A professor requires his students to write "God is dead" to take his philosophy class. He tells them that they won't meet the course requirement unless they do so. He says this because the students won't understand his philosophy class unless they deny the existence of God. But one student who believes in God refuses, saying, "I can't." The student is then warned that he will fail the class, which will affect his grades, and he won't be able to get a good job. His girlfriend also breaks up with him. He is tested to see if he still chooses faith. I remember watching such a movie.

Unfortunately, philosophy has largely become a worldly study that denies the other world, contrary to the time when it was first started by Socrates and Plato. This is very sad. It has become utilitarian and is caught up in just pursuing what a highly developed machine or computer would produce by processing certain data.

The test for the soul
on what to choose at the crossroads of life

• *Choice 1* Which do you save, your friend or five strangers on a track?

I have watched the philosophy classes of the famous Harvard professor, Michael Sandel, on TV. He poses the following question, for example. You are driving a train, and the track splits into two and you need to decide which way to go. On the right, your close friend is standing on the track alone. On the left, you see five strangers standing on the track. Which way would you turn the handle? It's too late to stop the train. Now, what do you do? It is a mean question, but he poses this question.

The answers are divided. You can't run over your close friend, so some of you would choose to go straight ahead to run over the five strangers. Others would think every life is equal and if it is one to five, one should die rather than five.

It is a little mean to ask such a question, but they do these kinds of thought experiments.

• *Choice 2* Which of the two drowning in the pond do you save?

There is another question: "You are rowing a boat. Two people are drowning in a pond. Which do you save?" One is your family member or a friend, and the other is a stranger; the question is which of the two to save.

Suppose you are rowing a boat and you see someone drowning. It is your mother. But on the other side, the prime minister is also drowning. Who do you save first?

From a public standpoint, you might feel that you must save the prime minister because a prime minister does a more important job than your mother. But you might also think, "Should I abandon my mother, who has raised me? Won't I regret this for the rest of my life? Even if the prime minister drowns, someone else should appear to take his place."

Which to choose is left to the judgment of each person at that time, but these internal conflicts are the ones that will be the materials to nurture one's mind in many ways.

• *Choice 3* Do you save the person who can't save themselves or the person who is close to you?

A similar conversation comes up in the movie *We Were There* by Director Takahiro Miki. The characters discuss, "If two people are drowning, do you save the one who doesn't have the power to save themselves and who wouldn't be saved unless you saved them or the one who is close to you and is important to you?" One of the main characters is then asked, "Why did you go for the other woman?" and his answer was, "She was 'sinking.' She can't save herself and she doesn't have anyone to save her, so I had to." And because he had chosen the other woman instead of the woman who had always been waiting for him, his friend says, "What are you talking about! The woman who's been waiting for you for five years is 'sinking' too!" For a movie about young love, it has some interesting dialogue. But in reality, it is not easy to tell if someone is really 'sinking' or not.

In life, there are many crossroads, such as "What will you abandon and what will you take?" "Which path will you give up and which path will you take?" These questions will appear over and over again, many, many times. You will face countless situations that will make you think, "If I had decided in this way, things wouldn't have turned out this way."

When you make a choice, more often than not, you have to let go of the other option. This is a very painful thing to do, but this is the "test of the soul" that is different from the tests you take at school.

• *Choice 4* Clashing values between faith and family

Here is another example. Suppose you finally found Happy Science faith. You feel, "These are true teachings and I want to follow them. But Happy Science is new and my parents do not know well about it. They tell me to stop being involved in it because new religions tend to be dangerous." If you are a student who came to the city from rural area, the parent might warn you by saying, "I'm going to stop sending you money if you get involved with this religion!" If the parents dislike religion in general, they might say, "I'm going to disown you. You're not my child anymore!" Cases like that can happen, and I imagine some people have experienced it.

There are also cases of a couple who didn't have a religious belief before marriage, but one of them comes to have faith after getting married. The other might think, "This was not the deal. The conditions have changed." A wife or a husband may come to have faith, while the other is a materialist or doesn't think well of religions. In such cases, even though nothing about their work has changed, or nothing about their family relationship has changed, the partner is now "a different person inside," so the other might demand that their partner stop being involved in a religion. It is actually one of the reasons for a couple to file for divorce at the family court in Japan. Should someone become so devoted to a religion that they neglect their family, the partner may bring them to court for a divorce. Freedom of religious belief is a constitutional right, but some people become so passionate that they neglect their wives or kids or abandon their husbands. This can become a very difficult battle of values.

The more passionately the person feels about their faith, the more coldly the people around them will regard them and say, "You're going to ruin your life." They say so not necessarily because they are mean but because they truly care about the person. So, this is a difficult issue.

3

The Battle between
Common Sense and Faith

Jesus demanded that
people choose faith over common sense

Based on Jesus' words, Christianity is generally thought to be a religion that preaches love and peace. But there were times when Jesus said something else. He said, "Do not think that I have come to bring peace to the earth. I have not come to bring peace, but a sword." He said he had come to tear apart wife and husband, parents and children, and family members and even to set them to fight against each other. So, he had come to bring a sword.

Whether a family will truly be torn apart depends on the case, and his words may not apply to every situation, but there will certainly be instances where a family becomes divided over faith. Even if a family is united through shared faith, other close families or relatives could be practicing a different faith, resulting in a "religious war." This could cause the families to decide that they can't get along with each other anymore. Things like this can happen. Or in a family that follows the same religion, if one of the family members quits, they can no longer stay together; they could end up living apart or filing for divorce.

Although Jesus Christ came to teach love and peace, there are people who can see the Truth and people who cannot. The people who believe they can see could actually be the ones who are "blind," whereas those who are regarded as being "oblivious of common sense," "careless about the customs," or "unaware of others' goodwill" could be seeing the Truth more clearly. Because of this, there may be times when you are faced with a difficult situation.

If you are an average person with an ordinary job and an ordinary home, or if you are satisfied with the faith at the level of the "fifth dimensional Goodness Realm," where you are just expected to be a good person who can get along with everyone else, then I think you can sheathe your sword and make compromises as you go through life. But someone who has a very strong sense of mission will not be satisfied with that level. If you sense your mission strongly and believe you have something to fulfill, then it will not be easy for anyone to stop you from going that way.

People like that will abandon all kinds of things. They will abandon all to choose the path of realizing the Truth. I suggest that you ask yourself if you are such a person.

You will also be tested. Will you be able to overcome adversities when you come up against them? Some will give up. Others will compromise. It is sad, but this cannot be helped.

For example, Happy Science built a school called Happy Science Academy, of which there is Nasu Main Campus in Eastern Japan and Kansai Campus in Western Japan. Many of its graduates go on to the Happy Science University that is also built by our organization, but in the past, they also went to other, regular universities. Sadly, of those who went to other universities, especially to the so-called prestigious schools, there are more who lost their faith or became doubtful of it.

This is because there are still far more people who do not have faith than those who do. You could stand in a position of "1 against 100" or "1 student against a class of 50." You could be the only person who believes in Happy Science whereas the remaining 49 do not. So, the more earnestly and loudly you act on your faith, the more isolated you could become. It could be too painful to bear that.

When a woman who is going through this is approached by a man who feels sorry for her, befriends her, and then becomes her lover, she might feel as if she has been saved, even if he is an atheist, or a materialist, or someone who is very worldly. Then, she might choose love and come to abandon faith. This really happens. Actually, it's quite common.

This is a matter of the percentage of people who have faith. A person's faith would be protected if surrounded by people of the same faith. But if you go to a place where people don't have faith, you might want to hide it like an underground Christian. Or you might reveal it little by little and try to get along well with others by accepting people's general values and maintaining an adequate distance. Some people may be flexible enough to behave like that. Even so, depending on how they act, there will still be moments when they stand out from the rest.

Shakyamuni Buddha worked to build social credibility when he clashed with the norms of society

Today, you would not be rejected in a job interview just because you are a Happy Science believer.

Back when I was working at a company, I was once involved in recruiting fresh graduates. I looked at the applicants' school grades and examined their characters through interviews. But in addition to that, applicants were checked by the inquiry agencies while they were still attending school.

A job interview was normally stretched out over three days. This was because, after about three days, the inquiry agencies were able to get back with the investigation report. When a company asked about specific students who were applying for a job, they could get the reports describing even the information about the students' circle of friends.

Even if the applicants were good candidates, there could be some issues with their friends. So, they were flagged A, B, C, D, E, and F according to the potential risk to the company. A, B, and C were fine, whereas D, E, and F indicated red flags. If they had a friend that might later pose a problem—for example, a best friend involved in left-wing revolutionary activities—then the report showed the risk that the applicant could be influenced after joining the company. The report also showed what the applicant had been doing as a student. It's amazing that the agencies looked up so many things.

They also investigated the applicants' religious beliefs. This is a story from when I was a recruiter of the company I worked for, so of course Happy Science had not existed yet, but they even found out whether a student was a member of Soka Gakkai, a Japanese religious group.

If the company hired someone unknowingly, they figured it out afterward. At the time, Soka Gakkai members visited their then-head temple Taisekiji on a set day every year. So, anyone who would take a day off from work that day had a circular mark on the calendar, and if the circle was drawn every year, they were marked with an "S," for Soka Gakkai, indicating he was a follower. The company investigated that far.

Some companies do not hire people who believe in particular religions.

In the case of Happy Science, there was already "Ryuho Okawa Book Study Club" even at the University of

Tokyo since as early as the 90s. This was around the time I gave my lecture "The Age of Daybreak" (given on May 26, 1991, at the University of Tokyo. Compiled in *The Royal Road of Life*). The names of the club's representatives could have certainly been identified, but it didn't seem to have affected them in finding a job at banks or government offices. It was obvious that Happy Science had gained society's trust from a relatively early stage. On seeing that belief in Happy Science did not have a negative impact on a person's employment, I felt that building a certain level of credibility was worth it. This is what I experienced.

Even so, there will surely be times when you clash with the values of this world and feel torn apart. Jesus was not the only one who experienced this. Shakyamuni Buddha did too.

In the beginning, Shakyamuni Buddha trained alone for six years before taking on five disciples. He then went to a nearby village to do missionary work, and a son of a wealthy man, Yasa, became a member. It is handed down that around this time, his followers expanded to 61. After a rich son who was said to have been wearing gold sandals joined, the other villagers began to come in, and the number of followers rapidly grew. I imagine people were enthusiastic about it, just like we see in new religions.

But soon, people began to complain. They said, "My son was supposed to succeed me but he left to join Shakyamuni's order" or "Once your children hear his lecture, they will renounce the world and never come back. So, be careful!" These stories began to circulate.

In today's terms, it became a bit of a social problem. The common practice in India at the time was to pass down the family estate to the eldest son. So, losing the family heir posed problems, and it was becoming an issue.

Even though families were large and had a lot of kids in those times, Shakyamuni Buddha decided to check if someone was not the first-born son who had to take care of his parents before allowing him to join the group of renunciants. And if that was the case, he told the first-born son to reconsider becoming a monk. He also set a condition: "The second son and younger may join the renunciant group with the permission of their parents." He drew the line in this way.

Anything that suddenly gains popularity in this world can sometimes be dangerous, so society tries to keep it in check. In that regard, Happy Science is a rare religion that talks about the importance of building trust.

The purer you become in your faith, the more you tend to feel like ignoring the matters of this world. But it is usually the matters of this world that trip you and bog you down. So, my hope is that you will also become smart in a worldly sense, to a certain degree. I wish you will be wiser as a human being.

Sometimes I wonder if we are too considerate for religion, but at different opportunities, I teach about wisdom for living in this world. As a way of living in this world, I often teach, "If you do this, this is how you will normally be judged." I also recommend that people make efforts, saying, "To grow fully as a human being means to become someone who can take responsibility for society. So, make the effort to be able to take responsibility in your relationships as well." I say this out of kindness, but I also understand that once you become really pure and spiritual, nothing of this world will matter to you anymore.

The antisocial religion Aum took advantage of the early case of the Buddhist order

As I read Buddhist books, I knew that in Shakyamuni's time, many people renounced the world to join his order, so society was harshly critical of his disciples. Even a song was made about it. That is why Shakyamuni Buddha became selective about who could join.

A Japanese religion named Aum, which started around the same time as Happy Science but became a criminal group, took advantage of the aspect that early Buddhism was seen as "antisocial." They encouraged many people to renounce the world to join their group, saying, "Even Shakyamuni Buddha was criticized by society, so it's OK that more and more people join us."

But what Aum did after making people join was strip them of all their property. They took everything people had, including bankbooks, savings, and name seals. In some cases, they burned people to ashes after that. Bad examples like this can be produced, so we must be careful.

Back in 1991, Happy Science held protests against the photo magazine articles of a specific publisher. The protests were repeatedly broadcast on TV and caused some commotion for about a year. But in *Shukyo Shimbun*, a religious newspaper that is said to be backed by a new Korean religious group, I read an article that was in favor of us.

It wrote something like, "The Bible says that when Jesus saw people selling and buying in the temple of God, he went furious and said, 'How dare you! I will not allow you to do business in front of my Father's house.' He overthrew the vendors' tables and drove their things away. In today's terms, this would be called 'obstruction of business.' Jesus did not hesitate to obstruct people's business, so we see nothing wrong with what Happy Science is doing." They showed their support in this way.

I felt grateful, but at the same time, I did not want us to be seen as birds of the same feather. The following year, the religion that backed the paper stepped out into society, assuming it was time for religions to be openly active, but they were then hammered on TV and withdrew a year later. By looking at the activities of Happy Science, they came out believing that religions were now welcomed by society, but they were struck down and hid again.

That was 1992. At that time, a commentator said in a talk show, "Now that we see next religious groups like the Korean one have come out, I feel bad for having criticized Happy Science last year." After that, I happened to sit near this commentator on a flight. When he noticed me, he looked embarrassed and said, "I have always carried this guilt that I may have done something wrong. After I criticized Happy Science, other religious groups like the Unification Church and Aum came out. On seeing these groups, I felt guilty for having criticized Happy Science."

Spreading the teachings
while building trust in this world

There are differences between religions. At Happy Science, we have adopted the stance, "The Truth is true and correct. We spread our teachings fair and square while trying to avoid social friction to some extent. We don't lie. We never deceive people to bring them in or use fakes to do that. We are always fair and square in the way we conduct our activities."

There are times when our activities are not recognized, but we are a religion that does not lie or deceive. We conduct ourselves properly. Also, since I worked in finance before I started Happy Science, I always feel we must be clear and reasonable with money and should not do anything illegal.

But sometimes there are disciples who make mistakes without realizing it. We are a large group, so there are times when we have members who do not understand the dos and don'ts of society. Even so, we have been told by various authorities that we are an organization that has caused very little trouble. The troubles are very few. With this many members, it would not be surprising for us to have a lot more trouble, but we have always been told we have relatively few.

In that sense, it might feel like we are being weighed down, slowing our momentum. But without the trust of this world, it will be hard to make worldly people believe, so we are making an effort as best as we can on this point.

I could "go off the rails" like Jesus, but I am holding back and spreading our teachings while building trust and foundations in this world. Even if we teach about the other world and spirits, they are invisible and many people cannot understand them either. We also talk about space people, so we might already appear eccentric to some. But our basic stance is to say what we believe is right, even after thinking about it logically and rationally. After seeing the way I have been and the way Happy Science has been for the past couple of decades, I think society has come to trust that we only say things we have perceived as true. In that sense, I am also trying to protect my followers.

4

Convey the Love of Your Lord God

Many people today think
love is something they take from others

I try to make these kinds of worldly efforts as much as I can, but there is something I need to finally mention. Watching the people who stumble and fail, I notice that sometimes it is because of financial issues but most often it is because of love.

The love we teach at Happy Science is the "love that gives." This is what we mainly teach. But when we say "love," people usually imagine it to be "love that takes." They are preoccupied with getting the object of their affection to love them.

However, if everyone were to take love, what would happen to the world? It would be as if in a marketplace, where many stores have their merchandise on display, everyone takes whatever they feel, "Oh, I want this," and walks off with it. I'm sure everyone has things they want, but they're required to pay for them and purchase them properly. You can't take something just because you want it. Of course, the situation wouldn't exactly be the same, but if everyone becomes a taker of love, then there wouldn't be any suppliers of love.

Give-and-take is still better than to just take; you are giving the same amount of what you received, and you can break even. But what I am saying here is that I want you to go beyond the level of give-and-take and realize "selfless love," or "sacred love," as much as you can.

Some people think you are stupid when you say, "Give love." They may think, "It is wiser to take. The more you can take cleverly, without others noticing, the smarter you are. That's why people try hard to go to a prestigious school and show off that brand name or go to a good company and boast about that brand name. You can pretend to be a son or daughter of a distinguished family. By doing all sorts of things like this, you can learn the skills to take the best for yourself from other people. That's what being smart is all about. You study and get good marks at school to advance in this world. If you are successful, you can gain status, power, the opposite sex, and the respect of society. Nothing but good can come out of that. This is why I'm studying just for myself. What's wrong with that?"

The love of the Savior who even stakes his own life

I believe it's good to study for yourself when you are young, but you shouldn't stay that way forever. You can focus on yourself until around age 30 at most. Until around 30 years of age, it's good to study for yourself, acquire a skill for yourself, take up hobbies and lessons, and do different things to increase your prestige because it can expand the range of your life experience. But after you pass the age of 30, you need to begin giving back to society.

Who you are today is the result of the love your parents have given you and the support your schoolteachers and other people in society have given you. So, why not make the remainder of your days a life of giving back? That's naturally the way we should live.

At that time, why not have something extra, beyond give-and-take? I believe that the more you give, the higher you will rise, while still alive, to be a resident of the fourth dimension or higher—a dimension that is not of this third dimensional world. What matters is your mind. However, some people just don't understand this.

In general, first comes love for your close family. You will have love toward someone close to you, such as your parents, child, spouse, and siblings. Such love for family and love for friends will come first. After that, you will gradually come to have love for the people who are farther away, love for your company or what makes up the community of today, and love for your country.

In the beginning, it often starts with personal love. So, in extreme cases, you may look like an egoist. But among the people who are recognized as "smart" because of their background, there are those who are egoists and those who are not. In the case of egoists, even if they are praised and admired as great in the beginning, people will soon stop praising them. For example, when they get good grades, graduate from a good school, pass a difficult certification exam, or start working at a prestigious company, they might first be told, "That's impressive." Things may go well until that point, but if they continue to study or work only to be praised or only for their own benefit, then they might receive some flattery, but nothing more.

On the other hand, virtue is born in people who devote themselves to the world and to other people, outside of the realm of give-and-take, and in those who believe they must use their talents in serving others. They do not do it to gain virtue but acquire it naturally.

As an example, please allow me to use American movies, a trilogy of Batman movies ("The Dark Knight Trilogy"). Batman is the son of rich parents, but his parents were killed. So, he strives to eradicate crime from the city. However, his home is burned, his company is lost, and he loses everything. His life is also put in danger. In the third movie, there is a scene where Cat Woman, who happens to become his sidekick, says, "Save yourself. You don't owe these people anymore. You've given them everything." But Batman says, "Not yet."

My wife likes this phrase and she reminds me of it from time to time. Batman says, "Not everything. Not yet." He not only fights the evil that was trying to take over Gotham City but also carries the neutron bomb that is about to explode over the bay using his flying vehicle, the Bat, which seemed to be on autopilot. The bomb explodes over the ocean, and the city is saved in the end.

Before that, he is told that he has lost everything, that he has done all he could, but Batman says, "Not yet." There, I see in him a type of Savior, depicted as an American hero.

So, in the end, you will go as far as to stake your own life. You need to understand this point.

The two important teachings Jesus taught

Jesus said the following when he was asked, "Which teaching is the most important of all?" Jesus taught many teachings, so one of his followers became confused and asked him, "Which is the great commandment in the law?" Jesus then answered, "You shall love the Lord your God. This is the first and great commandment." And when asked the second most important teaching, he answered, "You shall love your neighbor as yourself."

• 1) Love your Lord God

When you hear, "Love your Lord God," you might think God is an egoist. But that is not what it means. People who do not acknowledge God—in other words, who do not love God—cannot really love others. They can only love others for their own benefit, and they sometimes love others to use them. But love has nothing to do with egoists, and love is not just about giving out money.

Believing in God is the same as loving God. To believe in God is to love God.

God loves everyone, from those in the Spirit World to those living on earth. That is why God is working for the sake of love. And part of God's soul, or part of God's light, manifests as many Great Angels and other higher beings to be born on earth, and they devote themselves to the sacred work and carry out activities to save other people.

God's work can become greater if the number of people who believe in God increases. When more people believe in God, the work God can do to save people on earth will become much greater. That is why the most important teaching is to "Love God."

• 2) Love your neighbor

The second important teaching is "Love your neighbor."

To love someone who benefits you—such as a romantic partner, a spouse, parent or child, or friend or acquaintance—is standard moral behavior and not wrong. It's important on a moral level. But you must not be so bound by it that you neglect to love God. You must not let it get in the way of spreading the Truth or cause you to do nothing for the many people who fall to hell after they die.

Sometimes, even if you are aware that people are headed for hell, you may avoid telling them of the Truth out of worry that by doing missionary work, you'll be misunderstood, be persecuted, or suffer disadvantages at work. But that is not good. You must give love even to your neighbors who do not benefit you and the many people you meet in the course of your life.

Simply put, giving love is the same as practicing your faith in God.

God's teachings will spread
when you fully commit yourself to giving love

There is the phrase, "He who does not love does not know God." I believe these are the words of John. It is true; those who do not have love do not know God. To put it in another way, it means the egoists have no faith.

As I said earlier, anyone can become selfish naturally by birth. Insects and animals are all selfish. They self-centeredly search for food and self-centeredly think all the time about how to escape death.

Human beings are the same. Everyone is basically self-centered in their decisions. They do not know how to love others unless they are taught. Only after being taught do they learn it is what they must do.

They also never learn about the Spirit World, the world beyond this one, from just living in this world. People are blind to the Real World while they live. That's why Jesus often said that you are no different from a blind man who gropes in darkness.

Those who can truly see know about the future lives as well as the past lives and heaven and hell in the Spirit World. Imagine how many people will have to suffer in hell for hundreds of years, and you will naturally wish for them to read at least one book of Truth or listen to at least one lecture of Truth or one song of Truth while they are alive. This is what it means to love your neighbor.

To put it in another way, while loving God comes first, loving your neighbor is proof that you love God. By showing that you love someone who brings you no benefit, you are proving that you love God.

This is what Jesus taught.

Religion is not a business or a company. For a company, it might be sufficient to make enough money to pay their employees, although of course, it would be good to make more than that. A company could be happy just making enough to pay its employees and having excess to be saved.

But religion cannot be satisfied with that level. For example, people who need Happy Science are not just in Japan but every part of the world. Many countries are poor. In those countries, it is not easy for our members to collect money and build a temple on their own. However, problems will not be solved with money alone. Money allows a company to open a branch overseas, but that is not enough for a religion.

You must first love your Lord God, secondly, love your neighbor. Only when you commit yourself fully to this spirit of love will the teachings really spread. In other words, as more people believe in the teachings, supported by principles of economy and management in this world, the teachings will spread naturally.

If the teachings are not spreading, you may have a too business-like way of thinking, so you must correct that. It shows you are not yet fully convinced of how important these teachings are.

It is sad that your awareness is not strong enough.

In this world, sometimes one's academic level and school grades are valued instead of one's supremacy of faith. These are used as important titles and have replaced God, Buddha, tathagatas, and bodhisattvas. There are times when the name of the school people graduated from or their test scores are considered more important than anything else, but that is a shallow way of thinking.

God's teachings have been taught from an eternal past, whereas universities were built but about 100 years ago in Japan. So, they cannot replace God.

When we built Happy Science University, scholars from various private universities formed a council to discuss whether it qualifies as a proper university. But most of these council members did not even know that the best and oldest universities in the world all started as a seminary.

Universities such as Oxford University and Harvard University actually started as divinity schools. They were founded as a place to train monks who would preach the teachings of God. The teachers were monks there. This is how universities began. Over the course of hundreds of years, they turned into general universities, but Oxford, Harvard, and others were all formerly divinity schools. They were all "Happy Science University" in the beginning. They simply came to teach different subjects over the years. People seem to have forgotten how universities originally started, but they began with monks preaching the teachings of God.

People who did not know this formed a council and decided that Happy Science University is not qualified as a university, saying that its curriculum contains religious teachings or that spiritual messages are not academic studies. But if it were not for messages from spirits, or words from God, religion would not be born in this world in the first place. They do not understand this fundamental point.

The love of the Lord God that protects Earth and governs even the universe

Technologies and the sciences will probably continue to advance and make society more convenient. I don't intend to deny them, and it's fine to use them effectively.

Thanks to technology, my lectures now reach people in various ways through different media. They can be recorded and shown at different opportunities to more people. When transcribed, they can be made into a book. We can do these things because our modern age is advanced. I am grateful that we can do what could not be done in ancient times.

But then again, if you kneel before convenience and end up throwing away something that is of essential importance, then I must clearly tell you that you are making a mistake.

First, the Spirit World is the Real World.

At the top of it is God.

God is the Creator.

He created humankind as well as all kinds of living things,
And He created the history of Earth.

God sent and dispatched all kinds of people to this earth
To create different civilizations in different ages.

Caught in its currents,

People experienced both happiness and unhappiness,
And some might have drowned in the violent stream.

When the times were bad,

God worked to change those times as well.

There were many times when even God's messengers
Died in misery.

But through it all,

Not once did God's love ever stop flowing.

Happy Science also voices political and economic opinions.

These are the opinions coming from heaven, saying,

"Change the way the civilization in this world is."

So, please do not take them in the same way as
The opinions of ordinary scholars.

To love your Lord God is very important,
For the Lord God loves everyone more than anyone else.

Therefore, add power to God, and supply energy to God.
This is also one of the missions of human beings,
The children of God.
Those who do not have love do not know God.
Those who do not believe in God do not have love.
Those who do not know love do not understand the mind.
Those who do not understand the mind
Do not understand what spirits are.
Those who do not understand spirits
Cannot have faith and will not believe in God.
Everything is a cycle.
In this cycle, see God and the Spirit World
From the perspective of love,
And learn that people are connected by a line of light
That brings them together.
To take it a step further,
Earth does not exist just for itself.
Earth is not a planet just for earthlings.
Earth is not just for the creatures living on Earth.
It is not just for the animals and plants.
To this planet Earth too,
Many have come from other planets for soul training.
I know it is hard to believe.
But I want you to know that
It is also a precious love to protect this Earth
And maintain it as the soul's training ground.

Afterword

From Love to Love—this is the start and end of my Laws.

In between, I shall teach a lot about Truth and happiness.

Love your Lord God.

He is the Being who loves you the most.

Accept His Love with all your heart.

El Cantare is with you from the beginning to the end.

The Being is the Father and the Mother of your souls.

I love each and every one of you

Now and forever.

Ryuho Okawa
Master & CEO of Happy Science Group
November 2021

TRANSLATOR'S NOTE

1 Nichiren (1222-1282) was a Japanese Buddhist monk and the founder of the Nichiren school of Buddhism. In 1274 and 1281, Great Mongolia did actually attack Japan.

2 The Emperor Wu of Han (156-87 B.C.) was the seventh emperor of the Han dynasty in ancient China.

3 The First Emperor of Qin (259-216 B.C.) persecuted Confucians who criticized him and burned books of ideology.

4 Shimabara Rebellion (1637-1638) was an uprising mainly led by Japanese Christians.

5 Hideyoshi Toyotomi (1537-1598) was a Japanese warlord who succeeded in the unification of Japan.

6 Prince Shotoku (574-622) was a politician and a member of the Japanese Imperial family. Conflicts regarding whether or not to accept Buddhism occurred during his time, and the pro-Buddhist side won. He introduced Buddhism into politics.

7 Ryunosuke Akutagawa (1892-1927) and Yasunari Kawabata (1899-1972) were Japanese writers. Kawabata received the Nobel Prize in Literature.

8 Tao Yuanming (365-427) was a writer and poet in ancient China.

9 Ryoma Sakamoto (1836-1867) was a Japanese political activist in the later Edo period. He was involved in the political movement to overthrow the Tokugawa Shogunate and also was involved in the Meiji Restoration.

This book is a compilation of the lectures, with additions, as listed below.
They are English translations of the lectures originally given in Japanese.

- Chapter One -

Now, here, Elohim is thinking about.

Japanese title: *Elohim no Honshin*
Lecture given on July 11, 2021
at Grand Head Temple Shoshinkan of Happy Science,
Tochigi Prefecture, Japan

- Chapter Two -

What the Messiah Should Say and Do Now

Japanese title: *Ima, Meshia ga Kataru beki koto, Nasu beki koto*
Lecture given on July 18, 2021
at the Special Lecture Hall, Happy Science, Japan

- Chapter Three -

The Teachings of Messiah

Japanese title: *Meshia no Oshie*
Lecture given on July 21, 2021
at the Special Lecture Hall, Happy Science, Japan

- Chapter Four -

The Heart of the Earth

Japanese title: *Chikyu no Kokoro*
Lecture given on July 29, 2021
at the Special Lecture Hall, Happy Science, Japan

- Chapter Five -

The Love of Messiah

Japanese title: *Meshia no Ai*
Lecture given on August 4, 2021
at the Special Lecture Hall, Happy Science, Japan

For a deeper understanding of The Laws Of Messiah,
see other books below by Ryuho Okawa:

The Golden Laws [Tokyo, HS Press, 2015]

Secrets of the Everlasting Truths [Tokyo, IRH Press, 2012]

The Royal Road of Life [New York, IRH Press, 2020]

Spiritual Reading of Novel Coronavirus Infection Originated in China [Tokyo, HS Press, 2020]

The Xi Jinping Thought Now [Tokyo, HS Press, 2021]

On Carbon footprints reducing - Why Greta gets angry? [Tokyo, HS Press, 2020]

Nelson Mandela's Last Message to the World [Tokyo, HS Press, 2013]

The following book is only available at Happy Science locations. Please see the contact information on p. 230-231.

The Laws of Alpha [Tokyo, Happy Science, 2014]

ABOUT THE AUTHOR

RYUHO OKAWA was born on July 7th 1956, in Tokushima, Japan. After graduating from the University of Tokyo with a law degree, he joined a Tokyo-based trading house. While working at its New York headquarters, he studied international finance at the Graduate Center of the City University of New York. In 1981, he attained Great Enlightenment and became aware that he is El Cantare with a mission to bring salvation to all humankind. In 1986, he established Happy Science. It now has members in over 160 countries across the world, with more than 700 branches and temples as well as 10,000 missionary houses around the world. The total number of lectures has exceeded 3,350 (of which more than 150 are in English) and over 2,900 books (of which more than 600 are Spiritual Interview Series) have been published, many of which are translated into 37 languages. Many of the books, including *The Laws of the Sun* have become best sellers or million sellers. To date, Happy Science has produced 24 movies. The original story and original concept were given by the Executive Producer Ryuho Okawa. Recent movie titles are *Into the Dreams...and Horror Experiences* (live-action, August 2021), *The Laws of the Universe - The Age of Elohim* (animation movie, October 2021), *The Cherry Bushido* (live-action movie scheduled to be released in February 2022). He has also composed the lyrics and music of over 450 songs, such as theme songs and featured songs of movies. Moreover, he is the Founder of Happy Science University and Happy Science Academy (Junior and Senior High School), Founder and President of the Happiness Realization Party, Founder and Honorary Headmaster of Happy Science Institute of Government and Management, Founder of IRH Press Co., Ltd., and the Chairperson of NEW STAR PRODUCTION Co., Ltd. and ARI Production Co., Ltd.

WHAT IS EL CANTARE?

The God of the Earth El Cantare is the Primordial God of Earth's spirit group. He is the supreme existence whom Jesus called Father, and is *Ame-no-Mioya-Gami*, the Japanese Father God. El Cantare has sent down his branch spirits, such as Shakyamuni Buddha and Hermes, many times to guide humankind and develop many civilizations. Currently, the core consciousness of El Cantare has descended to Earth as Master Ryuho Okawa, and is giving teachings to unite various religions and to integrate various fields of study to guide all humankind to true happiness.

Alpha is a part of the core consciousness of El Cantare who descended to Earth around 330 million years ago. Alpha preached Earth's Truths to harmonize and unify Earth-born humans and space people who came from other planets.

Elohim is a part of El Cantare's core consciousness who descended to Earth around 150 million years ago. He gave wisdom, mainly on the differences of light and darkness, good and evil.

Ame-no-Mioya-Gami (the Japanese Father God) is the Creator God and the original ancestor of the Japanese people who appears in the ancient literature, *Hotsuma Tsutae*. It is believed that He descended on the foothills of Mt. Fuji about 30,000 years ago and built the Fuji dynasty, which is the root of the Japanese civilization. With justice as the central pillar, Ame-no-Mioya-Gami's teachings spread to ancient civilizations of other countries in the world.

Shakyamuni Buddha was born as a prince into the Shakya Clan in India around 2,600 years ago. When he was 29 years old, he renounced the world and sought enlightenment. He later attained Great Enlightenment and founded Buddhism.

Hermes is one of the 12 Olympian gods in Greek mythology, but the spiritual Truth is that he taught the teachings of love and progress around 4,300 years ago that became the origin of the current Western civilization. He is a hero that truly existed.

Ophealis was born in Greece around 6,500 years ago and was the leader who took an expedition to as far as Egypt. He is the God of miracles, prosperity, and arts, and is known as Osiris in the Egyptian mythology.

Rient Arl Croud was born as a king of the ancient Incan Empire around 7,000 years ago and taught about the mysteries of the mind. In the heavenly world, he is responsible for the interactions that take place between various planets.

Thoth was an almighty leader who built the golden age of the Atlantic civilization around 12,000 years ago. In the Egyptian mythology, he is known as god Thoth.

Ra Mu was a leader who built the golden age of the civilization of Mu around 17,000 years ago. As a religious leader and a politician, he ruled by uniting religion and politics.

ABOUT HAPPY SCIENCE

Happy Science is a global movement that empowers individuals to find purpose and spiritual happiness and to share that happiness with their families, societies, and the world. With more than 12 million members around the world, Happy Science aims to increase awareness of spiritual truths and expand our capacity for love, compassion, and joy so that together we can create the kind of world we all wish to live in.

Activities at Happy Science are based on the Principle of Happiness (Love, Wisdom, Self-Reflection, and Progress). This principle embraces worldwide philosophies and beliefs, transcending boundaries of culture and religions.

Love teaches us to give ourselves freely without expecting anything in return; it encompasses giving, nurturing, and forgiving.

Wisdom leads us to the insights of spiritual truths, and opens us to the true meaning of life and the will of God (the universe, the highest power, Buddha).

Self-Reflection brings a mindful, nonjudgmental lens to our thoughts and actions to help us find our truest selves—the essence of our souls—and deepen our connection to the highest power. It helps us attain a clean and peaceful mind and leads us to the right life path.

Progress emphasizes the positive, dynamic aspects of our spiritual growth—actions we can take to manifest and spread happiness around the world. It's a path that not only expands our soul growth, but also furthers the collective potential of the world we live in.

PROGRAMS AND EVENTS

The doors of Happy Science are open to all. We offer a variety of programs and events, including self-exploration and self-growth programs, spiritual seminars, meditation and contemplation sessions, study groups, and book events.

Our programs are designed to:
* Deepen your understanding of your purpose and meaning in life
* Improve your relationships and increase your capacity to love unconditionally
* Attain peace of mind, decrease anxiety and stress, and feel positive
* Gain deeper insights and a broader perspective on the world
* Learn how to overcome life's challenges
   ... and much more.

For more information, visit happy-science.org.

OUR ACTIVITIES

Happy Science does other various activities to provide support for those in need.

- **You Are An Angel! General Incorporated Association**
  Happy Science has a volunteer network in Japan that encourages and supports children with disabilities as well as their parents and guardians.

- **Never Mind School for Truancy**
  At 'Never Mind,' we support students who find it very challenging to attend schools in Japan. We also nurture their self-help spirit and power to rebound against obstacles in life based on Master Okawa's teachings and faith.

- **"Prevention Against Suicide" Campaign since 2003**
  A nationwide campaign to reduce suicides; over 20,000 people commit suicide every year in Japan. "The Suicide Prevention Website-Words of Truth for You-" presents spiritual prescriptions for worries such as depression, lost love, extramarital affairs, bullying and work-related problems, thereby saving many lives.

- **Support for Anti-bullying Campaigns**
  Happy Science provides support for a group of parents and guardians, Network to Protect Children from Bullying, a general incorporated foundation launched in Japan to end bullying, including those that can even be called a criminal offense. So far, the network received more than 5,000 cases and resolved 90% of them.

◆ **The Golden Age Scholarship**

This scholarship is granted to students who can contribute greatly and bring a hopeful future to the world.

◆ **Success No.1**
Buddha's Truth Afterschool Academy

Happy Science has over 180 classrooms throughout Japan and in several cities around the world that focus on afterschool education for children. The education focuses on faith and morals in addition to supporting children's school studies.

◆ **Angel Plan V**

For children under the age of kindergarten, Happy Science holds classes for nurturing healthy, positive, and creative boys and girls.

◆ **Future Stars Training Department**

The Future Stars Training Department was founded within the Happy Science Media Division with the goal of nurturing talented individuals to become successful in the performing arts and entertainment industry.

◆ **NEW STAR PRODUCTION Co., Ltd.**
ARI Production Co., Ltd.

We have companies to nurture actors and actresses, artists, and vocalists. They are also involved in film production.

CONTACT INFORMATION

Happy Science is a worldwide organization with branches and temples around the globe. For a comprehensive list, visit the worldwide directory at *happy-science.org*. The following are some of the many Happy Science locations:

UNITED STATES AND CANADA

New York
79 Franklin St., New York, NY 10013
Phone: 212-343-7972
Fax: 212-343-7973
Email: ny@happy-science.org
Website: happyscience-usa.org

New Jersey
Email: nj@happy-science.org
Website: happyscience-usa.org

Chicago
2300 Barrington Rd., Suite #400,
Hoffman Estates, IL 60169
Phone: 630-937-3077
Email: chicago@happy-science.org
Website: happyscience-usa.org

Florida
5208 8th St., Zephyrhills, FL 33542
Phone: 813-715-0000
Fax: 813-715-0010
Email: florida@happy-science.org
Website: happyscience-usa.org

Atlanta
1874 Piedmont Ave., NE Suite 360-C
Atlanta, GA 30324
Phone: 404-892-7770
Email: atlanta@happy-science.org
Website: happyscience-usa.org

San Francisco
525 Clinton St.
Redwood City, CA 94062
Phone & Fax: 650-363-2777
Email: sf@happy-science.org
Website: happyscience-usa.org

Los Angeles
1590 E. Del Mar Blvd., Pasadena, CA 91106
Phone: 626-395-7775
Fax: 626-395-7776
Email: la@happy-science.org
Website: happyscience-usa.org

Orange County
10231 Slater Ave., #204
Fountain Valley, CA 92708
Phone: 714-659-1501
Email: oc@happy-science.org
Website: happyscience-usa.org

San Diego
7841 Balboa Ave., Suite #202
San Diego, CA 92111
Phone: 626-395-7775
Fax: 626-395-7776
E-mail: sandiego@happy-science.org
Website: happyscience-usa.org

Hawaii
Phone: 808-591-9772
Fax: 808-591-9776
Email: hi@happy-science.org
Website: happyscience-usa.org

Kauai
3343 Kanakolu Street, Suite 5
Lihue, HI 96766
Phone: 808-822-7007
Fax: 808-822-6007
Email: kauai-hi@happy-science.org
Website: happyscience-usa.org

Toronto
845 The Queensway
Etobicoke ON M8Z 1N6 Canada
Phone: 1-416-901-3747
Email: toronto@happy-science.org
Website: happy-science.ca

Vancouver
#201-2607 East 49th Avenue
Vancouver, BC, V5S 1J9, Canada
Phone: 1-604-437-7735
Fax: 1-604-437-7764
Email: vancouver@happy-science.org
Website: happy-science.ca

INTERNATIONAL

Tokyo
1-6-7 Togoshi, Shinagawa
Tokyo, 142-0041 Japan
Phone: 81-3-6384-5770
Fax: 81-3-6384-5776
Email: tokyo@happy-science.org
Website: happy-science.org

Seoul
74, Sadang-ro 27-gil,
Dongjak-gu, Seoul, Korea
Phone: 82-2-3478-8777
Fax: 82-2-3478-9777
Email: korea@happy-science.org
Website: happyscience-korea.org

London
3 Margaret St.
London, W1W 8RE United Kingdom
Phone: 44-20-7323-9255
Fax: 44-20-7323-9344
Email: eu@happy-science.org
Website: happyscience-uk.org

Taipei
No. 89, Lane 155, Dunhua N. Road
Songshan District, Taipei City 105, Taiwan
Phone: 886-2-2719-9377
Fax: 886-2-2719-5570
Email: taiwan@happy-science.org
Website: happyscience-tw.org

Sydney
516 Pacific Highway, Lane Cove North,
2066 NSW, Australia
Phone: 61-2-9411-2877
Fax: 61-2-9411-2822
Email: sydney@happy-science.org

Kuala Lumpur
No 22A, Block 2, Jalil Link Jalan Jalil
Jaya 2, Bukit Jalil 57000,
Kuala Lumpur, Malaysia
Phone: 60-3-8998-7877
Fax: 60-3-8998-7977
Email: malaysia@happy-science.org
Website: happyscience.org.my

Sao Paulo
Rua. Domingos de Morais 1154,
Vila Mariana, Sao Paulo SP
CEP 04010-100, Brazil
Phone: 55-11-5088-3800
Email: sp@happy-science.org
Website: happyscience.com.br

Kathmandu
Kathmandu Metropolitan City,
Ward No. 15, Ring Road, Kimdol,
Sitapaila Kathmandu, Nepal
Phone: 97-714-272931
Email: nepal@happy-science.org

Jundiai
Rua Congo, 447, Jd. Bonfiglioli
Jundiai-CEP, 13207-340, Brazil
Phone: 55-11-4587-5952
Email: jundiai@happy-science.org

Kampala
Plot 877 Rubaga Road, Kampala
P.O. Box 34130, Kampala, Uganda
Phone: 256-79-4682-121
Email: uganda@happy-science.org
Website: happyscience-uganda.org

The Happiness Realization Party (HRP) was founded in May 2009 by Master Ryuho Okawa as part of the Happy Science Group. HRP strives to improve the Japanese society, based on three basic political principles of "freedom, democracy, and faith," and let Japan promote individual and public happiness from Asia to the world as a leader nation.

1) Diplomacy and Security: Protecting Freedom, Democracy, and Faith of Japan and the World from China's Totalitarianism

Japan's current defense system is insufficient against China's expanding hegemony and the threat of North Korea's nuclear missiles. Japan, as the leader of Asia, must strengthen its defense power and promote strategic diplomacy together with the nations which share the values of freedom, democracy, and faith. Further, HRP aims to realize world peace under the leadership of Japan, the nation with the spirit of religious tolerance.

2) Economy: Early economic recovery through utilizing the "wisdom of the private sector"

Economy has been damaged severely by the novel coronavirus originated in China. Many companies have been forced into bankruptcy or out of business. What is needed for economic recovery now is not subsidies and regulations by the government, but policies which can utilize the "wisdom of the private sector."

For more information, visit en.hr-party.jp

HAPPY SCIENCE ACADEMY JUNIOR AND SENIOR HIGH SCHOOL

Happy Science Academy Junior and Senior High School is a boarding school founded with the goal of educating the future leaders of the world who can have a big vision, persevere, and take on new challenges.

Currently, there are two campuses in Japan; the Nasu Main Campus in Tochigi Prefecture, founded in 2010, and the Kansai Campus in Shiga Prefecture, founded in 2013.

Nasu Main Campus

Kansai Campus

HAPPY SCIENCE UNIVERSITY

THE FOUNDING SPIRIT AND THE GOAL OF EDUCATION

Based on the founding philosophy of the university, "Exploration of happiness and the creation of a new civilization," education, research and studies will be provided to help students acquire deep understanding grounded in religious belief and advanced expertise with the objectives of producing "great talents of virtue" who can contribute in a broad-ranging way to serve Japan and the international society.

FACULTIES

Faculty of human happiness

Students in this faculty will pursue liberal arts from various perspectives with a multidisciplinary approach, explore and envision an ideal state of human beings and society.

Faculty of successful management

This faculty aims to realize successful management that helps organizations to create value and wealth for society and to contribute to the happiness and the development of management and employees as well as society as a whole.

Faculty of future creation

Students in this faculty study subjects such as political science, journalism, performing arts and artistic expression, and explore and present new political and cultural models based on truth, goodness and beauty.

Faculty of future industry

This faculty aims to nurture engineers who can resolve various issues facing modern civilization from a technological standpoint and contribute to the creation of new industries of the future.

ABOUT IRH PRESS USA

IRH Press USA Inc. was founded in 2013 as an affiliated firm of IRH Press Co., Ltd. Based in New York, the press publishes books in various categories including spirituality, religion, and self-improvement and publishes books by Ryuho Okawa, the author of over 100 million books sold worldwide. For more information, visit okawabooks.com.

Follow us on:

Facebook: Okawa Books   **Twitter:** Okawa Books
Goodreads: Ryuho Okawa   **Instagram:** OkawaBooks
Pinterest: Okawa Books

——— NEWSLETTER ———

To receive book related news, promotions and events, please subscribe to our newsletter below.

🐦 eepurl.com/bsMeJj

——— OKAWA BOOK CLUB PODCAST ———

A conversation about Ryuho Okawa's titles, topics ranging from self-help, current affairs, spirituality and religions. Available at iTunes, Spotify and Amazon Music.

BOOKS BY RYUHO OKAWA

RYUHO OKAWA'S LAWS SERIES

The Laws Series is an annual volume of books that are mainly comprised of Ryuho Okawa's lectures that function as universal guidance to all people. They are of various topics that were given in accordance with the changes that each year brings. *The Laws of the Sun*, the first publication of the laws series, ranked in the annual best-selling list in Japan in 1994. Since, the laws series' titles have ranked in the annual best-selling list every year for more than two decades, setting socio-cultural trends in Japan and around the world.

The 27th Laws Series
THE LAWS OF SECRET

AWAKEN TO THIS NEW WORLD
AND CHANGE YOUR LIFE

Paperback • 248 pages • $16.95
ISBN: 978-1-942125-81-5

Our physical world coexists with the multi-dimensional spirit world and we are constantly interacting with some kind of spiritual energy, whether positive or negative, without consciously realizing it. This book reveals how our lives are affected by invisible influences, including the spiritual reasons behind influenza, the novel coronavirus infection, and other illnesses.

The new view of the world in this book will inspire you to change your life in a better direction, and to become someone who can give hope and courage to others in this age of confusion.

For a complete list of books, visit <u>okawabooks.com</u>

THE TRILOGY

The first three volumes of the Laws Series, *The Laws of the Sun*, *The Golden Laws*, and *The Nine Dimensions* make a trilogy that completes the basic framework of the teachings of God's Truths. *The Laws of the Sun* discusses the structure of God's Laws, *The Golden Laws* expounds on the doctrine of time, and *The Nine Dimensions* reveals the nature of space.

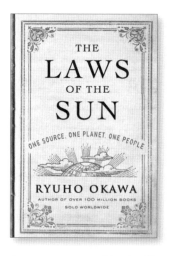

THE LAWS OF THE SUN

ONE SOURCE, ONE PLANET, ONE PEOPLE

Paperback • 288 pages • $15.95
ISBN: 978-1-942125-43-3

IMAGINE IF YOU COULD ASK GOD why He created this world and what spiritual laws He used to shape us—and everything around us. If we could understand His designs and intentions, we could discover what our goals in life should be and whether our actions move us closer to those goals or farther away.

At a young age, a spiritual calling prompted Ryuho Okawa to outline what he innately understood to be universal truths for all humankind. In *The Laws of the Sun*, Okawa outlines these laws of the universe and provides a road map for living one's life with greater purpose and meaning.

In this powerful book, Ryuho Okawa reveals the transcendent nature of consciousness and the secrets of our multidimensional universe and our place in it. By understanding the different stages of love and following the Buddhist Eightfold Path, he believes we can speed up our eternal process of development. *The Laws of the Sun* shows the way to realize true happiness—a happiness that continues from this world through the other.

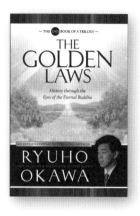

THE GOLDEN LAWS
HISTORY THROUGH THE EYES OF THE ETERNAL BUDDHA

Paperback • 201 pages • $14.95
ISBN: 978-1-941779-81-1

Throughout history, Great Guiding Spirits have been present on Earth in both the East and the West at crucial points in human history to further our spiritual development. *The Golden Laws* reveals how Divine Plan has been unfolding on Earth, and outlines 5,000 years of the secret history of humankind. Once we understand the true course of history, through past, present and into the future, we cannot help but become aware of the significance of our spiritual mission in the present age.

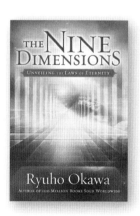

THE NINE DIMENSIONS
UNVEILING THE LAWS OF ETERNITY

Paperback • 168 pages • $15.95
ISBN: 978-0-982698-56-3

This book is a window into the mind of our loving God, who designed this world and the vast, wondrous world of our afterlife as a school with many levels through which our souls learn and grow. When the religions and cultures of the world discover the truth of their common spiritual origin, they will be inspired to accept their differences, come together under faith in God, and build an era of harmony and peaceful progress on Earth.

For a complete list of books, visit okawabooks.com

NEW BOOKS

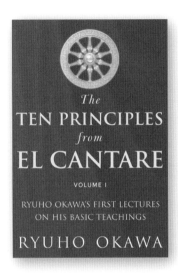

THE TEN PRINCIPLES
FROM EL CANTARE VOLUME I

RYUHO OKAWA'S FIRST LECTURES ON HIS BASIC TEACHINGS

Paperback • 232 pages • $16.95
ISBN: 978-1-942125-85-3

This book contains the historic lectures given on the first five principles of the Ten Principles of Happy Science from the author, Ryuho Okawa, who is revered as World Teacher. These first five lectures produced an enthusiastic fellowship in Happy Science Japan and became the foundation of the current global utopian movement. It starts with the historic lecture, "The Principle of Happiness," in which Okawa delivered "The Fourfold Path" of *Love, Wisdom, Self-reflection* and *Progress*. By living "The Fourfold Path," you will attain true happiness and start on your path to enlightenment.

For a complete list of books, visit okawabooks.com

240

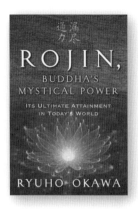

ROJIN, BUDDHA'S MYSTICAL POWER

ITS ULTIMATE ATTAINMENT IN TODAY'S WORLD

Paperback • 232 pages • $16.95
ISBN: 978-1-942125-82-2

In this book, Ryuho Okawa has redefined the traditional Buddhist term *Rojin* and explained that in modern society it means the following: the ability for individuals with great spiritual powers to live in the world as people with common sense while using their abilities to the optimal level. This book will unravel the mystery of the mind and lead you to the path to enlightenment.

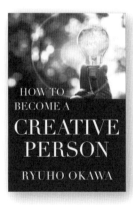

HOW TO BECOME A CREATIVE PERSON

Paperback • 176 pages • $16.95
ISBN: 978-1-942125-84-6

How can we become creative when we feel we are not naturally creative? This book provides easy to follow universal and hands-on-rules to become a creative person in work and life. These methods of becoming creative are certain to bring you success in work and life. Discover the secret ingredient for becoming truly creative.

For a complete list of books, visit okawabooks.com

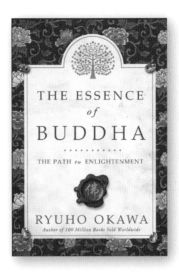

THE ESSENCE OF BUDDHA

THE PATH TO ENLIGHTENMENT

Paperback • 208 pages • $14.95
ISBN: 978-1-942125-06-8

In this book, Ryuho Okawa imparts in simple and accessible language his wisdom about the essence of Shakyamuni Buddha's philosophy of life and enlightenment–teachings that have been inspiring people all over the world for over 2,500 years. By offering a new perspective on core Buddhist thoughts that have long been cloaked in mystique, Okawa brings these teachings to life for modern people. *The Essence of Buddha* distills a way of life that anyone can practice to achieve a life of self-growth, compassionate living, and true happiness.

For a complete list of books, visit <u>okawabooks.com</u>

THE TRUE EIGHTFOLD PATH

GUIDEPOSTS FOR SELF-INNOVATION

Paperback • 272 pages • $16.95
ISBN: 978-1-942125-80-8

This book explains how we can apply the Eightfold Path, one of the main pillars of Shakyamuni Buddha's teachings, as everyday guideposts in the modern-age to achieve self-innovation to live better and make positive changes in these uncertain times.

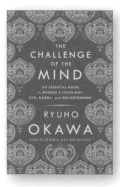

THE CHALLENGE OF THE MIND

AN ESSENTIAL GUIDE TO BUDDHA'S TEACHINGS: ZEN, KARMA AND ENLIGHTENMENT

Paperback • 208 pages • $16.95
ISBN: 978-1-942125-45-7

In this book, Ryuho Okawa explains essential Buddhist tenets and how to put them into practice. Enlightenment is not just an abstract idea but one that everyone can experience to some extent. Okawa offers a solid basis of reason and intellectual understanding to Buddhist concepts. By applying these basic principles to our lives, we can direct our minds to higher ideals and create a bright future for ourselves and others.

THE LAWS OF GREAT ENLIGHTENMENT

ALWAYS WALK WITH BUDDHA

Paperback • 232 pages • $17.95
ISBN: 978-1-942125-62-4

Constant self-blame for mistakes, setbacks, or failures and feelings of unforgivingness toward others are hard to overcome. Through the power of enlightenment we can learn to forgive ourselves and others, overcome life's problems, and courageously create a brighter future ourselves. This book addresses the core problems of life that people often struggle with and offers advice on how to overcome them based on spiritual truths.

For a complete list of books, visit okawabooks.com

THE LAWS SERIES

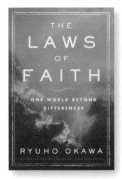

THE LAWS OF FAITH

ONE WORLD BEYOND DIFFERENCES

Paperback • 208 pages • $15.95
ISBN: 978-1-942125-34-1

Ryuho Okawa preaches at the core of a new universal religion from various angles while integrating logical and spiritual viewpoints in mind with current world situations. This book offers us the key to accept diversities beyond differences to create a world filled with peace and prosperity.

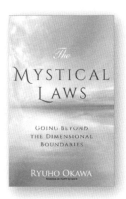

THE MYSTICAL LAWS

GOING BEYOND THE DIMENSIONAL BOUNDARIES

Paperback • 250 pages • $14.95
ISBN: 978-1-941779-48-4

"I believe that once you have finished reading this book, you will find it impossible to return to your old self, for you have now learned the secrets that run through this world and the other.

When you have learned of what has been hidden, will you feel guilt or will you find courage welling up from within?"

-From the Afterword

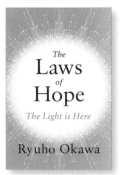

THE LAWS OF HOPE

THE LIGHT IS HERE

Paperback • 224 pages • $16.95
ISBN:978-1-942125-76-1

This book provides ways to bring light and hope to ourselves through our own efforts, even in the midst of sufferings and adversities. Inspired by a wish to bring happiness, success, and hope to humanity, Okawa shows us how to look at and think about our lives and circumstances. He says that hopes come true when we have the right mindset inside us.

For a complete list of books, visit okawabooks.com

RECOMMENDED BOOKS

THE STRONG MIND

THE ART OF BUILDING THE INNER STRENGTH
TO OVERCOME LIFE'S DIFFICULTIES

Paperback • 192 pages • $15.95
ISBN: 978-1-942125-36-5

The strong mind is what we need to rise time and
again, and to move forward no matter what difficulties
we face in life. This book will inspire and empower
you to take courage, develop a mature and cultivated
heart, and achieve resilience and hardiness so that you
can break through the barriers of your limits and keep
winning in the battle of your life.

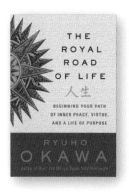

THE ROYAL ROAD OF LIFE

BEGINNING YOUR PATH OF INNER PEACE,
VIRTUE, AND A LIFE OF PURPOSE

Paperback • 224 pages • $16.95
ISBN: 978-1-942125-53-2

With over 30 years of lectures and teachings spanning
diverse topics of faith, self-growth, leadership (and more),
Ryuho Okawa presents the profound eastern wisdom
that he has cultivated on his approach to life. The Royal
Road of Life illuminates a path to becoming a person of
virtue, whose character and depth will move and inspire
others towards the same meaningful destination.

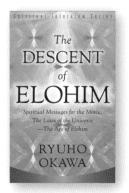

THE DESCENT OF ELOHIM

SPIRITUAL MESSAGES FOR THE MOVIE,
THE LAWS OF THE UNIVERSE-THE AGE OF ELOHIM

Paperback • 160 pages • $11.95
ISBN: 978-1-943928-17-0

This book contains the spiritual messages from Elohim,
the Lord who appears in the Old Testament and who
actually led His people about 150 million years ago.
Through this book and the movie, The Laws of the Universe
- The Age of Elohim, you can learn how life on Earth was
like at that time, and how diverse people, who had come
from other planets, fought each other until they finally
found peace and harmony under Lord Elohim.

For a complete list of books, visit <u>okawabooks.com</u>

SPIRITUAL WORLD 101
A Guide to a Spiritually Happy Life

MY JOURNEY THROUGH THE SPIRIT WORLD
A True Account of My Experiences of the Hereafter

THE HELL YOU NEVER KNEW
And How to Avoid Going There

TWICEBORN
My Early Thoughts that Revealed My True Mission

WORRY-FREE LIVING
Let Go of Stress and Live in Peace and Happiness

THE REAL EXORCIST
Attain Wisdom to Conquer Evil

THE HEART OF WORK
10 Keys to Living Your Calling

BASICS OF EXORCISM
How to Protect You and Your Family from Evil Spirits

HEALING FROM WITHIN
Life-Changing Keys to Calm, Spiritual, and Healthy Living

MUSIC BY RYUHO OKAWA

El Cantare Ryuho Okawa Original Songs

A song celebrating Lord God

A song celebrating Lord God,
the God of the Earth,
who is beyond a prophet.

❍ Will be released in January 2022

DVD
CD

The Water Revolution

English and Chinese version

For the truth and happiness of the 1.4 billion people in China who have no freedom. Love, justice, and sacred rage of God are on this melody that will give you courage to fight to bring peace.

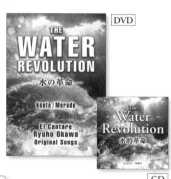

DVD

CD

Search on YouTube

the water revolution for a short ad!

Listen now today!

 Download from
Spotify iTunes Amazon

DVD, CD available at amazon.com,
and Happy Science locations worldwide

247